Also from Rhodes and Rose and published by Hardy Perennial Press:

MY Findings by Stu Cranstence

http://rhodesandrose.com
www.youtube.com/user/doctorodub
hardyperennialpress.com

ISBN# 978-1-7325402-5-5

Hardy Perennial Press LLC
1645 W. Valencia rd #109-154
Tucson AZ 85746

THE RHODES AND ROSE
Lifestyle Digest

By
Noel Rhodes and Owen Rose

Dedication

We would like to dedicate this book to all of our fans.

Introduction

As always, the holidays are just around the corner, so if you're going to outdo what you did last year, you better get started early.

Here at Rhodes and Rose we make the holidays last and last with our brand new Lifestyle Digest. This Digest is designed to help people find the goods and services that make life worth living. Each of the companies featured here have been thoroughly researched and their products and services have been personally tested by us before we recommend them to the general public. We have also included excerpts from the pages of the The Metro Daily Times Gazette Bugler to keep our readers informed.

This Lifestyle Digest will surely become a treasured resource for anyone looking to improve their daily lives with the latest and greatest in products and services. We hope you come to feel as passionately about these companies and individuals as we do.

In the back of the digest you will find a list of titles of all of the Rhodes and Rose videos on YouTube that pertain to many of the products and services offered here.

Thank you,
Noel Rhodes
Owen Rose

Comments on Rhodes and Rose videos

Comments on the Flextrek Whipsnake:
"There are very few videos better than this. Very, very few."
"A true classic."
"This is my all time favorite YouTube video."
"I love people that go to the effort to make this kind of nonsense. Hilarious."
"This is gold. So well written and produced."
"This is one of the best videos on YouTube."
"Funnier than anything SNL has done in the last 20 years."
"Watched this after 3 dabs and legit thought I was going to die."
"Honestly the funniest video I have ever seen."
"I want to have this shown on my funeral."
"This is so profoundly funny. I have watched this 20 times."
"Oh dear god I don't think I've ever laughed this hard."
"Literally the best thing I've ever seen in my life."
"This is one of the most hilarious videos I've ever seen. Absolute genius."
"I just laughed so hard I quit breathing....epic...tears."
"I'm crying and just laugh-choked."
"This is one of the funniest things I've seen on the Internet."
"This is genius. So funny. You've made me laugh so much...Thank You."
"This is the kind of stuff that propels humanity forward."

Comments on the Juggernaut Pharmaceutical Collection:
"So basically, if you take Stryreechlinstral...better get your affairs in order."
"Absolute genius."
"This one of the best things on YouTube. Kudos."
"As someone who was seriously damaged by a prescription drug, I find this to be too close to the truth. And funny as hell."
"Probably one of the best videos on YouTube."
"I think this is my favorite video on the internet."
"Amazing. I love these commercials."
"Somebody award the creator a Nobel prize."

Comment on Lorb Lorbson:
"This is art of the highest form."

Comment on Steg Prongsten and Kelp:
"I am so glad I've seen this. I feel complete."

Contents

Chapter One

Brought to you by the Flextrek 37,000,000,000,000

Your old backpack is good enough, right? You've had it for years and it always seemed to get the job done. It never let you down. Yeah your old backpack is good enough...right?

Yeah, that's world renowned naturalist and lecturer, the outdoors ultimate enthusiast, **STEVE CLIMBER**. That pack he's wearing is the Archwood Flextrek 37,000,000,000,000 - the **ZXYVR M**-Series Magnum Package.

SIMPLY MORE
The ultimate bulking agent

Do you get off the toilet seat and say to yourself, I'm producing stool, but it's not enough, I want more?

Founder Hugh Brown

"Believe me. I've been there, and I've developed a product that will **blow you away!**
It's called **Simply More**, and it's a bulking agent that's going to leave you *staring in wonder*. I didn't think it was possible to produce this kind of volume in such a short time.
After a few short weeks on my product line you'll be testing the handling capacity of your facilities too."

For more information, please LOG ON.

WhAT DO I WANT?

SIMPLY MORE

The Metro Daily Times Gazette Bulgler

When you've got to know, you know where you've got to go

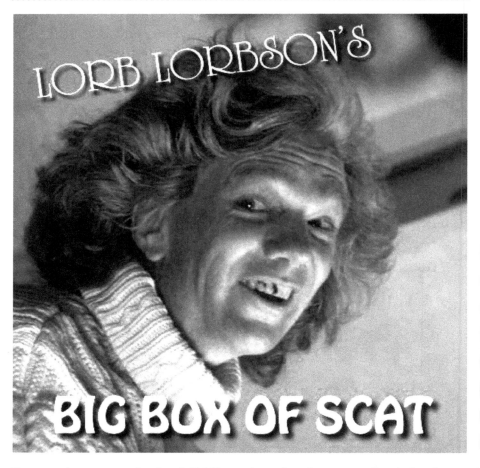

Do you love scat singing? Well so does local crooner Lorb Lorbson. He has just released a CD collection called Lorb Lorbson's *"Big Box of Scat"* that features scat versions of some of the greatest music of all time. Lorb scats his way through the soft rock hits of the 80s and the 90s in this 5 CD box set. People tend to get pretty excited when they hear what Lorbson does to their favorite songs.

The *"Big Box of Scat"* contains every take from the lengthy recording sessions. These tapes were thought to be intentionally destroyed, but renowned musical archivist, Ron Cranstence, rediscovered them in his shed and has remastered them.

You can catch Lorb Lorbson in person down at the legendary Cheripintera every Monday from 3:30-4:00 pm for his Twilight Series perfomances.

Hey guys!

Did you realize that by the year 2030, 80% of American men will have had male enhancement surgery? So simply having enlargement surgery **may not be enough.** Are we suggesting that you **not** have penis enlargement surgery? **Of course not!** We encourage and provide all male enhancements procedures. What we **are** saying, is that *it may not be enough*. Check out all the surprising new options in our new brochure.

Call the Male Adequacy Clinic today.

Satisfied customer - J.F.

Think of how bad you feel already, and think of how bad you'll feel if you get left **even further behind**.

The Male Adequacy Clinic

Thanks Juggernaut!

I used to suffer from vague feelings of unease (VFS), but then I asked my doctor about **Stryreechlinstral**. He said that with *proper diet and exercise* - and **Stryreechlinstral** - I could get back on track, doing the things I really want to do.

STRYREECHLINSTRAL

"I'm not letting the symptoms of VFS get between me and my dreams."

Juggernaut Pharmaceuticals

Stryreechlinstral is not for everyone.
Contact your physician if you experience:
Sudden dissolving of the teeth, withering of the brain cortex, aggressive clot-worm clusters in the ear canal, daytime night terrors, rapid snap-coiling of the penis (RSC), long periods of organ failure (also known as Corpse Syndrome), uncontrollable homicidal urges, foul smelling cauliflower-shaped growths on the anus and face, internal tissue lique-faction, testicular gigantism in men and women, butcher's hack - some-times called Coughing Up Bones, loud cracking of the nipples, early onset mortality, unexpected localized calcified growths (also known as an anus rib), weak stream.
Nursing mothers should stop nursing so that they can take **Stryreech-linstral** without killing their child. If you're taking **Stryreechlinstral** with **Myscleetra**, ask your doctor about taking **Clinflairtrynsol**.

With Stryreechlinstral I'm back on track, and back to doing the things I really want to do.

You're one tough customer.
You're the kind of guy that is really great.
No one's going to tell YOU what to do.

And you use

ЈEP+ACUA 7.000
Finally a razor with seven blades.

The Metro Daily Times Gazette Bulgler

When you've got to know, you know where you've got to go

"When the clacking is done making their beaks so sharp, well, that's when they come after you."

NOW YOU KNOW
WITH STU CRANSTENCE

The Metro Daily Times Gazette Bugler is happy to announce that a new columnist has joined our team. Stu Cranstence is a self-taught scientist, geologist, and anthropologist. His "Now You Know" column will inform readers about any number of fascinating subjects.

Hello. I'm Stu Cranstence. If you know anything about mountain lions you know that the sharpness of their beaks makes it very easy for them to peck out people's eyes. But most people don't know how they keep them so sharp.
*The most common method used by mountain lions is clacking. We've all heard the clacking of beaks in areas where mountain lions nest. When the clacking is done making their beaks so sharp, well, that's when they come after you. It's really amazing how little most people know about these **monsters of the deep**.*

Now you know!

Did you recently have to have your face and spinal chord removed after taking the drug Stryreechlinstral?

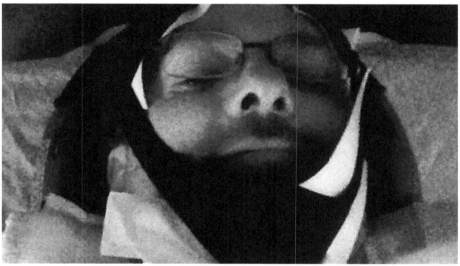

Actual client undergoing treatment

If so, you may be eligible for financial compensation.

$$$$$$$$$$$$$$

Contact the law offices of Ernst Ernst Ernst & Ernst immediately for information that will get you the help you deserve. All of our clients are people like you who are seeking financial relief to pay for the astronomical medical debt that is typical for Juggernaut customers.

CALL NOW!
1 (555)-ERNSTERNSTERNSTANDERNST

The law offices of
ERNST ERNST ERNST & ERNST

Let me think, does Steve Climber wear a backpack that he doesn't know is better than anybody else's?

I don't think so.

What about the Stealth Sass-Flex - DAY PACK - Eazee Breez Edition, L-SERIES?

I can't think of why anyone would want this pack...
oh, unless they wanted features like the Ridgitek Handstrut
Stabilizing Stiffener Rod - J-SERIES!

an act of desperation
the heart of the wolf is rain
an ancient new scent
the heart of the wolf is strong
tonight we run free
we'll be together

Wolfheart
The heart of a wolf
A new cologne for men

SIMPLY MORE

The ultimate bulking agent

Are you getting all that you want to out of yourself?

Founder Hugh Brown

"I want to ask you, *are you satisfied?* **Simply More** is a bulking agent that can expand your personal waste production at a rate you've only dreamed of.

You don't have to settle for the average ordinary output that so many people seem to just accept.

Just take **Simply More** bulking agent products with every meal. When you wake up in the morning, you'll be ready to produce, and at a volume that's going to *blow you away.*"

No training is needed!

Don't take our word for it.
Just ask **Simply More** user **Seth P.**
*"I used to walk away from the bathroom so disappointed, and I thought there wasn't anything I could really do about it. I started on the **Simply More** products, and within a couple of days...it was show time!"*

WHAT DO I WANT?
SIMPLY MORE

Chapter Two

Brought to you by Juggernaut Pharmaceuticals

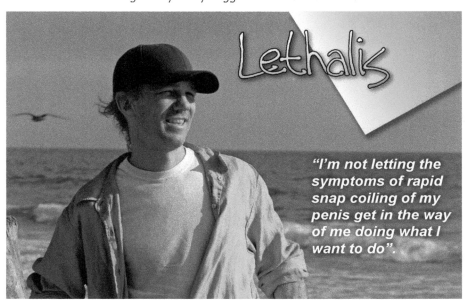

Lethalis

"I'm not letting the symptoms of rapid snap coiling of my penis get in the way of me doing what I want to do".

I used to suffer from vague feelings of unease. My doctor suggested I try **Stryreechlinstral**. Not everyone who uses **Stryreechlinstral** experiences Rapid Snap Coiling of the Penis. Most women do not...

I did.

My doctor told me that with **Lethalis**, my RSC could be **controlled** and **monitored**. Of course RSC can never be cured, but with *proper diet and exercise* - and **Lethalis** - **frequency and intensity** of episodes can be reduced (in some patients).

Lethalis is not for everyone.
Contact your physician if you experience:
Vague feelings of unease, giant eye-maggots, collapsing of the skull, a tendency to physically harm others, hardening of the heart, quivering or jumping scabs (also called Hell's Nightmare), boring thoughts, inability to move or breathe, inappropriate feelings towards ducks, development of taste buds in the colon, weak stream. Pregnant women who are taking **Lethalis** who are not considering suicide, should consider it, and should ask their doctor why they're taking **Lethalis**. If you're taking **Lethalis** with **Infectisol**, ask your doctor about taking **Poisantin**.

With Lethalis, I'm back on track, and doing the things I want to do.

Did you recently grow a third or fourth skeleton after taking the Juggernaut Pharmaceutical medication Lethalis?

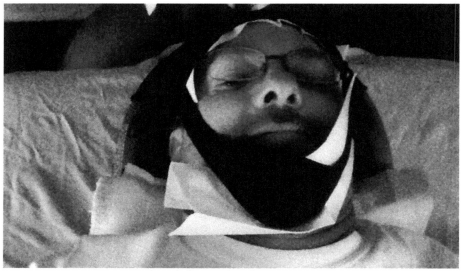

Actual client undergoing treatment

If so, you may be eligible for financial compensation.

$$$$$$$$$$$$$

Contact the law offices of Ernst Ernst Ernst & Ernst immediately for information that will get you the help you deserve. Our lawyers deal exclusively with claims against Juggernaut Pharmaceuticals, and that's why, according to Economy Magazine, we are the second fastest growing company in the world after Juggernaut Pharmaceuticals. You can get the financial relief you need to pay the astronomical debt that is typical for Juggernaut customers.

CALL NOW!
1 (555)-ERNSTERNSTERNSTANDERNST

The law offices of
ERNST ERNST ERNST & ERNST

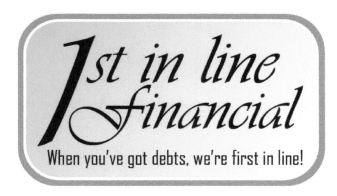

Hey guys!

Check out our new catalog of possibilities.
See pictures of our latest developments:

- Multiples
- Entwined multiples
- Implanted interior flexorods with ratchet sound

Also heavy-duty motorized carts that can be strapped on the front to solve your transport problems.

Call the **Male Adequacy Clinic** today.

Satisfied customer - J. F.

Think of how bad you feel already, and think of how bad you'll feel if you get left **even further behind.**

The *Male Adequacy Clinic*

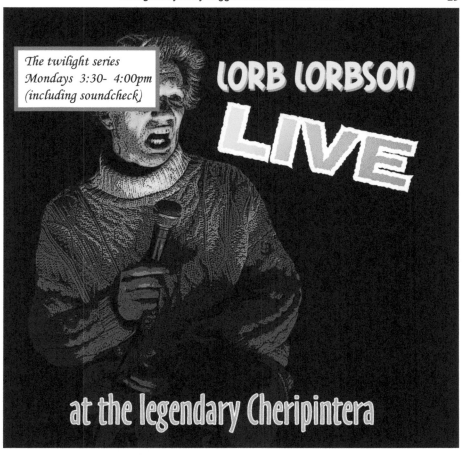

The twilight series
Mondays 3:30- 4:00pm
(including soundcheck)

LORB LORBSON LIVE

at the legendary Cheripintera

The timeless classic now in a collector can series

Pet Chef

Horse Chunks & Cheese

"You're dog is insane! For Pet Chef!"

The Metro Daily Times Gazette Bulgler

When you've got to know, you know where you've got to go

"Did you ever notice that no two people have ever seen a shooting star at the same time?"

NOW YOU KNOW
WITH STU CRANSTENCE

Shooting Stars:

Shooting stars are a myth. They don't exist. They are an optical illusion that exists in the human eye, most commonly in the osiris and the cornea (or corner of the eye to the layman). Did you ever notice that no two people have ever seen a shooting star at the same time?

Endangered Birds:

Many areas have endangered birds. The problem is that most people don't know which birds are endangered and which are safe birds. By the time they figure it out their eyes have already been pecked out.

Caution: Safe birds are the same in appearance as endangered birds! In one widely documented case an entire town was taken over by endangered birds. One family took shelter in their house but when the woman went into the attic the birds broke through a window and attacked her. The man came up and was able to save her but her eyes were nearly pecked out. This happened so long ago that it was in black and white.

Now you know!

You're no fool.

You're tough. You're not afraid to let people know where you stand

You don't let people push you around, OR tell you what to do.

And when you shave you use

SEPTACUA 7,000

Finally a razor with seven blades

So you're still wearing that old backpack, huh?

It's always been good enough, and good enough is good enough...right?

WRONG!

Once again, that's **Steve Climber**, world renowned naturalist and lecturer, the outdoors ultimate enthusiast, and once again he's wearing the Archwood Flextrek 37,000,000,000,000.

Only now he's rocking Archwood's newest model;

the **Flextrek 37,000,000,000,000**

AUGMENTEON

Welcome to planet girth

The Flextrek 37,000,000,000,000 expanded Augmenteon unit combines capacity with flexiblity and strenth.

There's only one pack that has this much more than everything you need.

This monumental Flextrek model offers the ultimate in durability and control, **even when fully engorged.**

Archwood introduces new options, like the *Wild Anteater Pull-Back Retracto-Hood - Q-Series.*

Every pack we make comes equipped with lubricated swivel-shaft contour action and our trademark

Purple-Vein Sheathing System - LS-Edition   V-Series.

Feel the rhythm of the trail with cutting edge Senso-Plugs

Go ahead, devastate the environment. You deserve it.

Humiliate your surroundings with the *Flextrek 37,000,000,000,000*

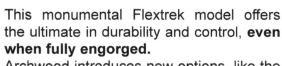

The #1 nation is havin' a celebration
Have a ball with Cren
When you're pumpin' iron
Or playing frisbee too
Celebrate with Cren
Celebrate with a friend
Thumbs up baby and turn it around
Cren is a big hit.
Why don't you read about it.
Do you get the picture baby? Click!
Roll on down to the #1 sound
And grab an ice cold Cren
At the disco, when you're moving to the beat.
And when you're rockin' Yow!
And movin' your feet
Celebrate with Cren
Rock out
You look cool on the slopes
But this brew is a blue chipper
Compute it all out and it reads CREN

Another fine product from Deal With It Brewery

#1

CREN
Beer

America's havin' a party!

Celebrate with Cren

SIMPLY MORE
The ultimate bulking agent

Wouldn't you like to test the limits of what you can get out of yourself?

Founder Hugh Brown

*"I know that when I walk out of a bathroom, I want to feel like I left something behind, so I developed **Simply More**.*
When I saw the terrific boost it gave to my personal output, I knew I wanted to share my secret with the world."

Why be satisfied with the ordinary?

Don't take our word for it.
Just ask **Simply More** user
Silvia P.
"My husband was very skeptical, but when I showed him what I was doing, he had to try the products, and now he's in some kind of exponential zone. It's unbelievable!"

No training is needed. To get started just LOG ON.

WHAT DO I WANT?
SIMPLY MORE

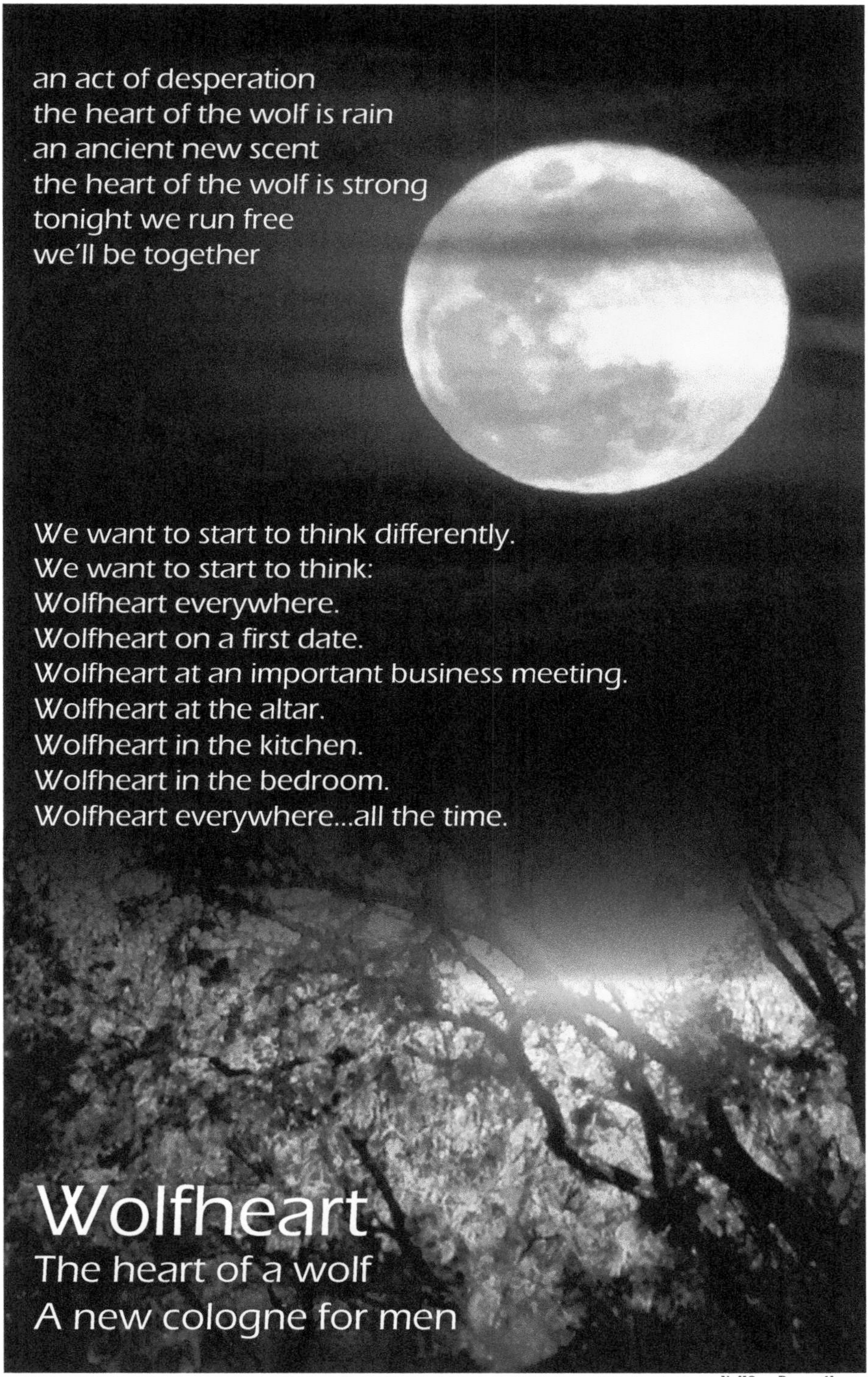
an act of desperation
the heart of the wolf is rain
an ancient new scent
the heart of the wolf is strong
tonight we run free
we'll be together
We want to start to think differently.
We want to start to think:
Wolfheart everywhere.
Wolfheart on a first date.
Wolfheart at an important business meeting.
Wolfheart at the altar.
Wolfheart in the kitchen.
Wolfheart in the bedroom.
Wolfheart everywhere...all the time.
Wolfheart
The heart of a wolf
A new cologne for men

NailGun Promotions

Thanks Juggernaut!

"Now I'm the one in control of the taste buds in my colon."

With Poisantin, I'm back to doing the things I really want to do.

I'm busy making my dreams come true, so when I developed taste buds in my colon - or TBIMC - I knew it was time to talk to my doctor. I used to suffer from rapid snap-coiling of my penis, or RSC, as a result of taking **Stryreechlinstral** to treat my vague feelings of unease. Thanks to **Lethalis**, now I'm in control of my RSC, and my RSC episodes aren't as frequent and intense, in some cases. Not everyone who takes **Lethalis** develops taste buds in their colon...

I did.

So I asked my doctor about **Poisantin**. Of course I know that my TBIMC can never be cured, but my doctor told me that with *proper diet and exercise* and **Poisantin**, my TBIMC could be monitored, putting **me** in control of the size and sensitivity of the taste buds in my colon.

Poisantin is not for everyone.

Contact your physician if you experience:

Vague feelings of unease, rapid snap-coiling of the penis, unexplained disappearance of the lungs, overwhelming amounts of ear wax (sometimes called bucket-of-muck), general body foaming with stench, absence of vital signs, non-stop funny bone (also known as not funny), hatred towards mockingbirds, galloping vertebrae (also known as the case for assisted suicide), weak stream, excessive hair growth inside the esophagus (sometimes called the **Poisantin** diet). If you're taking **Poisantin** as an appetite suppressant, ask your doctor about **Nauseantasol**. In rare cases, some people report development of a fourth and fifth nostril. Nursing mothers should have to sit in a special area, separate from the general public. Women taking **Poisantin** while trying to get pregnant, should ask their doctor about preparing for an ankle pregnancy.

Do you have an esophagus growing on your forehead after taking the Juggernaut Pharmaceutical medication Poisantin?

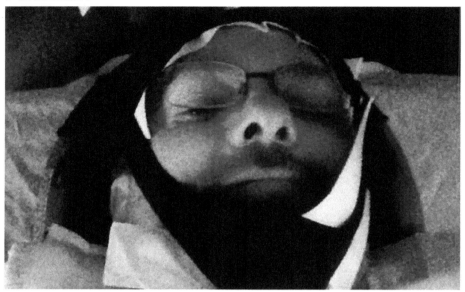

Actual client undergoing treatment

If so, you may be eligible for financial compensation.

$$$$$$$$$$$$$

Contact the law offices of Ernst Ernst Ernst & Ernst immediately for information that will get you the help you deserve. A judge has ruled that Juggernaut's claim that it ran out of room to list all of the side effects on the Poisantin package does not release them from liability.

All of our clients are people like you, seeking financial relief to pay for the astronomical debts that are typical for Juggernaut customers.

CALL NOW!
1 (555)-ERNSTERNSTERNSTANDERNST

The law offices of
ERNST ERNST ERNST & ERNST

𝕿𝖍𝖊 𝕸𝖊𝖙𝖗𝖔 𝕭𝖆𝖎𝖑𝖞 𝕿𝖎𝖒𝖊𝖘 𝕲𝖆𝖟𝖊𝖙𝖙𝖊 𝕭𝖚𝖑𝖌𝖑𝖊𝖗

When you've got to know, you know where you've got to go

In recent years yogo has become very popular, but most people don't know a damn thing about it.

First of all, yogo is over a hundred years old. It was invented by the ancient Egyptians. Back then, nobody spoke English. They only spoke Chinese. That's why it's called yogo.

Questions about yogo moves:

Why are they called jumping jacks?

No one knows why they are called jumping jacks. Why do you think scientists are studying it in the first place?

Why are women not allowed to be yogo instructors?

Can you imagine if women were allowed to be yogo instructors? Nag! Nag! Nag! Day and night! Night and day! That's why there are no women yogo instructors.

Stay Science!

The Metro Daily Times Gazette Bulgler

When you've got to know, you know where you've got to go

ATHLETE STEG PRONGSTEN TO TRAIN ON LOCAL BEACH

The Metro Daily Times Gazette Bugler has learned that Steg Prongsten will be doing an extended workout on a local beach. Prongsten, who describes himself as a "world-class athlete who's been traveling the globe looking for the ultimate settings to train and test the limits of human fitness," decided that a beach that the local population calls Evil Queen Beach would be just the ticket.

"This beach is a perfect training site. I'm going to get right to it - start training immediately," said Prongsten.

This remote beach is seldom visited as local legend has it that the kelp found on this beach once dominated the planet, ruled by a vicious queen. The legend states that the kelp almost wiped out all human life on earth, but were put into a 10,000 year sleep by a shaman's curse. These millions of kelp continue to sleep, unless someone breaks the shaman's curse, and wakes up the Queen.

*"I always train in my underwear. Because of the intensity of my workouts, I find it **critical** that I change my underwear frequently."*
Steg Prongsten

Your dog is more than just a pet.
Your dog is part of the family.

Here at Pet Chef we are constantly developing products to **extend the life of your dog. Dogjevity** is a supplement that can add **years and years** to the life of your dog!

You've seen all the gimmicks come and go. The flashes in the pans.

You don't really have time for the Johnny-come-latelys and the fancy frills.

You just want the best.

And when you shave you use

SEPTAQUA 7000

Finally a razor with seven blades

Chapter Three

Brought to you by Simply More- the Ultimate Bulking Agent

We don't care about the world.
We don't care about the universe.
We don't care about eternity.
We just care about ...you.

Juggernaut
Pharmaceuticals

Year after year Juggernaut Pharmaceuticals
has been working to take over your
world. Won't you join us?

"This thing performs like a dream. You can't even believe you've got a pack on."
Steve Climber

Flextrek 37,000,000,000,000

Archwood is proud to announce a breakthrough in backpack technology. Each of our new backpacks will ship with the Gravitrex anti-gravity module as standard equipment. This module is so advanced. When you're out on the trail it actually neutralizes gravity with a series of gyroscopic influations inside the module. You'll never feel anything like it. Don't embarrass yourself by being on the trail with anything other than the Archwood Flextrek 37,000,000,000,000 Gravitrex edition

Gravitrex

It actually neutralizes gravity.

SIMPLY MORE
The ultimate bulking agent

Founder Hugh Brown

When you leave the bathroom, don't you want to know you've left your mark?

*"Years ago when I developed **Simply More** I knew that I, like so many others, wanted to find a way to increase the small amount of stool I was producing.*
*I had no idea that today **Simply More** would be helping thousands of others get more and more out of themselves everyday."*

By taking Simply More with every meal, anyone can turn the ordinary into something REALLY big.

*Now available with **accelerator** for when your busy schedule demands it!*

*Try the new Ladies Formula - the same **Simply More** quality ingredients, but in a lavender package.*

Some training recommended.
To get started just LOG ON.

WHAT DO I WANT?
SIMPLY MORE

"If you're going to get too far into debt, we want you to do it with us."

*It's scary when you get too far into debt,
and if you're going to get too far into debt
we want you to do it with us.*

*We know more about working with people
and their debts than anyone.*

We can help you to start using those maxed-out credit cards again.

Vacations! Clothes! Cars!
It's all waiting for you!

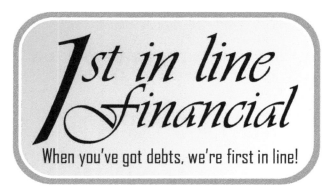

1st in line financial

When you've got debts, we're first in line!

If the question is: convenience

If the question is: ease of operation

If the question is: comfort

The answer is always the same

The Flextrek 37,000,000,000,000 remains the only backpack that anyone should buy

INTIMIDATE YOUR SURROUNDINGS

Our convenient training courses fit to *YOUR* schedule - professional training that's so convenient, you'll be on the trail when *YOU'RE* ready.

Finally *YOU'RE* the one who's in charge of the performance of your pack.

What about our patented U-Strut construction?

You know what you're doing. You don't need anybody to tell you that Archwood is the best.

It's about time somebody finally "got it" and put YOU back in charge. Maybe coming out on top is too much for the other guy to expect, but for you it's a way of life.

It's called just being smart.

ARCHWOOD

What about the Flextrek easy-adjusting **CLIC** method?

Talk about ease of use!

The **CLIC** method is as easy as it's spelled

Cut

Loosen

Insert

CLIC!

measure
extend
tape
hammer
O-Ring adjust
do-over,

and GO!

The Metro Daily Times Gazette Bulgler

When you've got to know, you know where you've got to go

LORBSON PRODUCES SCAT SAMPLE
FANS EAT IT UP

Local crooner Lorb Lorbson has released a scat version of Barbra Streisand's timeless classic, *The Way We Were*. Readers can scat along in their heads to the well-known melody. If people want to hear how Lorb treats beloved classic tunes they can head down to the legendary Cheripintera on Mondays from 3:30 - 4:00 pm, or they can buy tickets on the Princess Behemoth cruise to Mexico and Bermuda. Lorbson will be performing daily in the Juggernaut Theatre.

The Way We Were Scat

Squee-dap,
Squeeda skwoop dap dooba-doo
Squeeda skwap dowm deeboo deebow
Scooda deep dop squow

Squeep-dow,
Squeeda dap-dap squadap squap
Squeedup squadup squadup squady
Squeeda squap dow squoo

Squeeda squap-dap squeepa doop dap
Squeeba-doop dap squoo
Squeed Squeedap squooda squow
Skoo-doo-doo squap-dap sqouny squow doo squow
Squeedup squow-dow
Skoo-dow

Squee-dow,
Squap dap squeeda squada squoo
Skoota squowda squap-dow squap dow
Squa-da-dup squeedap squabba-squoo
Scoop squap scap squeep squap
Squee-dap squap squoo-dow
Squap squeedap scaddup squeee-dow
Squee squap squa squeee
Squa-dap sta squap

Lorbson has been a fixture at the legendary Cheripintera for decades. As part of his pre-gig routine, he always has a big plate of their classic spinach pesto.

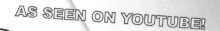

Thanks Juggernaut!

"I know I'll always have giant eye-maggots, but now I'm able to control the size and aggressiveness of them."

When I developed giant eye-maggots as a result of taking **Lethalis**, I knew it was time to talk to my doctor. I used to suffer from rapid snap coiling of my penis (RSC). My doctor said it was a result of taking **Stryreechlinstral** to help me deal with my vague feelings of unease. He also told me that with proper *diet and exercise* and **Lethalis**, my RSC episodes could be monitored and in some cases, made less severe and debilitating. Not everyone who uses **Lethalis** will develop giant eye-maggots...

I did.

So I asked my doctor about **Pandemical**, and he told me that with proper *diet and exercise* and **Pandemical**, my giant eye-maggots could be **monitored**, putting me in control of their size and aggressiveness (in some cases).

Pandemical is not for everyone.

Contact your physician immediately if you experience:

Vague feelings of unease, rapid snap-coiling of the penis, multiple facial scrotums, late night barking of the inner ear, male genital withering resulting in a micro-penis followed by severe shrinkage of the micro-penis, one really long tooth, compulsive scat singing, fast growing coarse whiskers on the pupils, re-routing of the intestines (also called an ass-nose), an uncontrollable urge to eat plywood, an ability to smell your brain, fire-worms in the naval, spontaneous nudism followed by projectile diarrhea, weak stream, decomposition of the body, crotch coral, continual percussive flatulence lasting more than a week, fundamentalist extremism, strong stream.

People taking **Pandemical** who have had braces will notice their teeth snapping back in to their original position.

If you're taking Pandemical with Lethalis, ask your doctor about taking Myscleetra and Sklinflairtrynsol.

Do you ever ask yourself, what is Steve Climber wearing?

Thanks for asking!

It's the Archwood **French Wedge**

This active wear combines state-of-the-art, cutting-edge fabrics with the ancient wisdom of the shepherds of the French Alps. Working in remote regions, the old French shepherds understood that in the humid French summers, washing becomes pointless. The French Wedge uses **unfathomable technology** to bond the inevitable fluids and substances with the fabric of the wedge, **actually increasing its strenth and durability** over time.

Detached hair follicles in ordinary active wear provide nothing but a nuisance, but did you know that

human hair is over 1,000 times stronger than steel?

Now that strenth can be put to use, bonding and reinforcing the French Wedge fabric structure with your every step.

What about odors?

If there's any company out there innovative enough to solve that problem, you can bet it's Archwood.

We're working on it!

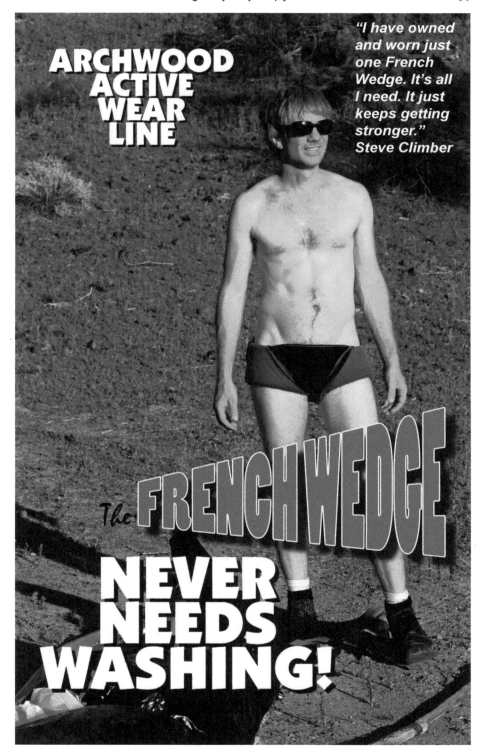

Have you lost all hope, become overwhelmed by a deep cynicism and profound self-loathing and compounded by a boiling reservoir of rage that threatens to explode at any moment after taking the Juggernaut medication Pandemical?

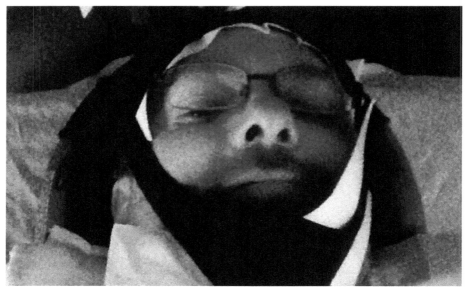

Actual client undergoing treatment

If so, you may be eligible for financial compensation.

$$$$$$$$$$$$$$

Ernst Ernst Ernst & Ernst is the ***world's largest and most powerful*** law firm in the world because it deals ***exclusively*** with claims against Juggernaut Pharmaceuticals.

Contact the law offices of Ernst Ernst Ernst & Ernst immediately for information that will get you the help you deserve.

CALL NOW!

1 (555)-ERNSTERNSTERNSTANDERNST

The law offices of
ERNST ERNST ERNST & ERNST

The Metro Daily Times Gazette Bulgler

AREA MAN BATTLES GIANT EYE-MAGGOTS

Local amateur scientist, author and lecturer Stu Cranstence was recently photographed with several large maggots that had emerged from the corner of his eye. While on his scientific expeditions, Cranstence has been forced to bring a paper bag to collect and dispose of them.

Cranstence says that the giant eye-maggots are merely a nuisance, and that he is currently taking the Juggernaut Pharmaceutical drug Pandemical to manage them.

"These are the giant eye-maggots. I think that's from taking the Stryreechlinstral - or was it Lethalis? Now I'm the one that's in control of the size and aggressiveness of them. Still a little aggressive though," insists Cranstence.

Climb Aboard!!
the Princess Behemoth

Holiday Caravan Cruises to Mexico and Bermuda

This cruise is going to be DYNAMITE!
Celebrities and corporate sponsors are lining up for this cruise.
- **Steve Climber from Archwood**
- **Hugh Brown from Simply More**
- **Steg Prongsten will be training on the upper deck**
- **Juggernaut Pharmaceuticals**
- **Pet Chef**
- **Stu Cranstence**
- **Lorb Lorbson**
- **Septaqua 7,000**
- **That guy from the Juggernaut ads will be there**
- **First in Line Financial**

NailGun Promotions will be giving away free opportunities to purchase products!
Stay tuned. More celebrities and corproate partners are signing up every day. If you're a Simply More enthususiast, this is a cruise you won't want to miss.

You love your dog!
Your dog is great!

But you don't want your dog to live for **too** long.

Here At Pet Chef, we've developed a dietary supplement that will actually *shorten the life of your dog!*

Dognity allows you to regulate the amount of time your dog will be impacting your life.

Don't let your dog hang around so long that the love you feel turns to disgust and loathing.

Let your dog die, with *Dognity*.

(Be sure to read all labels carefully)

Brought to you by Cren Beer

(Cren is not currently available)

ℭℌe ℳetro Daily ℭimes ℭazette Bulgler

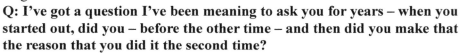

When you've got to know, you know where you've got to go

A reporter from the Metro Daily Times Gazette Bugler recently had a chance to sit down for an interview with local crooner Lorb Lorbson at the Legendary Cheripintera.

Q: Do you have a time slot that you play?

LL: The people at the Cheripintera said we're going to let you perform onstage. This is a public venue and they allow me to get up there in front of other people. As a performer that's worth a lot. I'll never let go of that. It's my time slot. Well it's an open slot, but I call it my slot.

Q: What time of day is it?

LL: It's the Monday afternoon slot.

Q: Like 3:00?

LL: It's later than that. It's 3:30 sometimes. Sometimes 3:45. I call it the twilight slot. It's a magic hour.

Q: I've got a question I've been meaning to ask you for years – when you started out, did you – before the other time – and then did you make that the reason that you did it the second time?

LL: Thanks, that's a great question. I love performing here.

Q: Do you have any special rituals you like to do before you perform?

LL: If you're going to the Cheripintera, you order the spinach pesto, that's just what you do. It's a special place. I'll never say anything but positive things - including about my fans here, the people that come out and see me.

Q: You've got that one fellow that really seems to be enthusiastic.

LL: There is a man that, yes, that man that comes here. He's here at a lot of the shows actually. He's a fan, so I have only positive things to say about him. I keep it positive when I talk about that man.

Q: He seems to know your material really well.

LL: He knows it well. He's the type of person that really wants to be closely involved in what you're doing. He wants to be a part of it.

That man

Q: So how do you feel about the sound man? Is there a little tension there?

LL: No. I have a sense that he's into my music, so that makes it a whole different dynamic. As far as the sound goes, my remarks are going to stay positive. Some sound people, it's like they're just going through the motions, other ones seem like they kind of get into the music. I think he's really kind of into my sound. He's the sound man. He really is.

John the sound man

Q: Do you have any other shows you're doing in town right now?

LL: Other places that I play other than the Cheripintera?

Q: Yes.

LL; Well I do play other places.

Q: Other live music venues?

LL: Yeah, I do. Or, I will. Right now the concentration is on the twilight series that I'm playing right now. That's what I'm focusing on, but the other places certainly are on the horizon...like a star.

Q: Have you built up a following over the years?

LL: You know it's really in flux right now. It's changing. Sometimes it's up, sometimes it's down. Right now it's down, but you know what that means, that it's coming back up anytime. Probably soon.

Q: So attendance has been down?

LL: Yeah, and down is part of up, really, because down is the part of up that's the best part, for me.

𝕮𝕳𝖊 𝕸𝖊𝖙𝖗𝖔 𝕯𝖆𝖎𝖑𝖞 𝕿𝖎𝖒𝖊𝖘 𝕲𝖆𝖟𝖊𝖙𝖙𝖊 𝕭𝖚𝖑𝖌𝖑𝖊𝖗

When you've got to know, you know where you've got to go

Medical Minute question for Dr. Soily Kruebens.

Mrs. E. writes,
*"Hi Doctor, I've been using **Simply More** for more than a year now, with great results. But lately, well, they seem a little ropey, if you know what I mean. I tried the accelerator, which helped because when they're ropey it can take too long. Is there something else I can do?"*

Dr. Soily Kruebens;
*"What you need to do is get yourself some **Simply More with Girth**. **Simply More with Girth** is a new product that they've come up with for people like yourself who have tried to solve the ropey problem. Using accelerator won't solve the ropey-ness, but **Simply More with Girth** will.*
*So what about combining the accelerator and the girth formulas? That's where the training comes in. **Simply More** trainers are standing by to help you with that."*

WhAT DO I WANT?

SIMPLY MORE

(training and a physician's prescription required in some areas)

If you're going to get too far into debt, we want you to do it with us.

America has seen some tough times. You've seen some tough times. You're up to your neck in debt and you're sinking fast, but you know that now is not the time to slow down. Your country depends on your spending to keep it strong and free. We're doing our part by creating a new line of credit, The Patriot's Pride Card.

The Patriot's Pride Card will allow you to accelerate your level of spending.

Our nation is counting on you. Don't let us down. Call today.

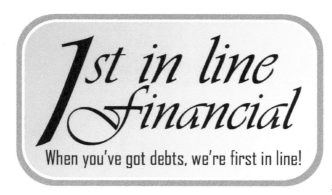

1st in line financial

When you've got debts, we're first in line!

AS SEEN ON YOUTUBE! **Juggernaut** Pharmaceuticals

Panacea

WITH NEW EXCITING ADDITIVES!

1 hour
Maximum strenth
Read all directions carefully.

"Not everyone who takes Pandemical will develop Crotch Coral, ...I did." **Stu Cranstence**

ARTIFICIALLY FLAVORED   12 CHEWABLE TABLETS 27500mg each

DIRECTIONS:
TAKE ONE PANACEA TABLET EVERY HOUR ON THE HOUR TO TREAT YOUR CROTCH CORAL. IF YOU MISS A DOSE, TAKE THREE DOUBLE DOSES THE NEXT HOUR. DO NOT EXCEED 434 TABLETS IN ANY 24 HOUR PERIOD. DO NOT CONSUME ALCOHOL WITHIN 51 DAYS OF TAKING PANACEA . OFF LABEL USES OF PANACEA ARE NOT RECOMMENDED. MANY MEN TAKING PANACEA MAY EXPERIENCE DETACHMENT OF THE GENITALS DURING INTERCOURSE (CONTACT YOUR DOCTOR IMMEDIATELY). WHILE PANACEA CAN NEVER CURE YOUR CROTCH CORAL, WITH PROPER DIET AND EXERCISE, AND PANACEA, YOU CAN CONTROL THE SIZE AND JAGGEDNESS OF YOUR CROTCH CORAL.

SIDE EFFECTS MAY INCLUDE(BUT ARE NOT LIMITED TO): VAGUE FEELINGS OF UNEASE (VFS), RAPID SNAP COILING OF THE PENIS (RSC), TASTE BUDS IN THE COLON (TBIMC), GIANT EYE MAGGOTS (GEM), MORE BORING THOUGHTS, WAY TOO MANY LEGS, NO MORE SKIN, LARYNX BIRDS, LEAPING DANDRUFF, TOES EVERYWHERE, DONKEY LAUGHING IN YOUR SLEEP, POOH ON YOUR ELBOW, WEAK STREAM, STRONG STREAM, JERKY TONGUE, CONSULT YOUR PHYSICIAN IMMEDIATELY IF YOUR SINUSES BECOME PACKED WITH TICKS, AS THIS MAY BE A SIGN OF A MORE SERIOUS CONDITION, WOMEN TAKING PANACEA SHOULD ANTICIPATE EXPERIENCING ALL OF THESE CONDITIONS ONLY MORE SEVERELY.

Panacea
Juggernaut Pharmaceuticals

ASK YOUR DOCTOR ABOUT ALL THE LATEST MEDICATIONS FROM JUGGERNAUT

WARNING!

THIS MEDICATION IS NOT APPROVED BY THE AMERICAN MEDICAL ASSOCIATION AND CARE SHOULD BE TAKEN WHEN USING THIS PRODUCT. THERE HAVE BEEN NUMEROUS REPORTS OF SERIOUS MEDICAL INJURIES AND DEFORMITIES RESULTING FROM THE USE OF THIS PRODUCT. JUGGERNAUT PHARMACEUTICALS IS NOT LICENSED IN THE UNTIED STATES TO ADMINISTER MEDICATIONS OF ANY KIND. THE ACTIVE INGREDIENTS IN THIS PRODUCT HAVE NOT BEEN TESTED BY THE FEDERAL DRUG ADMINISTRATION AND ARE NOT APPROVED FOR ANY TYPE OF USAGE WHATSOEVER. THE ACTIVE INGREDIENTS IN THIS PRODUCT ARE UNKNOWN TO THE STATE OF CALIFORNIA. THE OWNERS OF JUGGERNAUT PHARMACEUTICALS ARE WANTED BY FEDERAL, STATE AND LOCAL LAW ENFORCEMENT OFFICIALS FOR QUESTIONING ABOUT ILLEGAL PRACTICES. THIS PRODUCT HAS PROVEN TO BE HIGHLY ADDICTIVE. CARE SHOULD BE TAKEN. THIS PRODUCT SHOULD NOT BE TAKEN BY SENIORS, INFANTS, CHILDREN UNDER 15 YEARS OF AGE, ADULTS WHO HAVE HAD A PROBLEM WITH SUBSTANCE ABUSE AND ALL OTHERS.

WHILE TAKING **PANACEA**, IT'S VERY IMPORTANT THAT YOU KEEP A DETAILED DAILY LOG OF ALL OF YOUR BOWEL MOVEMENTS(WITH PHOTOGRAPHS, VIDEO, AND SAMPLES) AND BE SURE TO HAND DELIVER YOUR COLLECTIONS TO YOUR DOCTOR REGULARLY. ASK YOUR DOCTOR IF YOU ARE HEALTHY ENOUGH TO ENGAGE IN VERY UNUSUAL SEXUAL ACTIVITIES. **THIS MEDICATION IS EXTREMELY HABIT FORMING** PLEASE USE CAUTION. DO NOT COMBINE WITH SKINFLAIRTRYNISOL. ASK YOUR DOCTOR ABOUT ALL THE GREAT NEW MEDICATIONS FROM JUGGERNAUT!

IF YOU ARE TAKING PANACEA WITH MYSCLEETRA, ASK YOUR DOCTOR ABOUT SKLINFLAIRTRYNSOL
QUESTIONS? GO TO http://rhodesandrose.com/?page_id=456 WARNING: CONTAINS PHENYLALANINE

Thanks Juggernaut!

"I know I'll always have crotch coral, but now, thanks to Panacea, I'm back in charge - doing the things I want to do - making my dreams come true."

I'm busy making my dreams come true, so when I found out that I had crotch coral, I knew it was the perfect time to ask my doctor about **Panacea**. My doctor told me that my crotch coral was a result of taking **Pandemical** for the giant eye-maggots which were caused by **Poisantin** which I take to control the size and sensitivity of the taste buds in my colon that began emerging after I started taking **Lethalis** which put me in charge of my rapid snap-coiling penis that I first noticed after I started taking **Stryreechlinstral** to help me deal with my vague feelings of unease. Not everyone who takes **Pandemical** will develop crotch coral...

I did.

My doctor told me that with proper *diet and exercise* and **Panacea** I could *monitor* and *control* the size and jaggedness of my crotch coral. At first I was unsure about asking my doctor about my crotch coral. At first I didn't want to talk to my doctor about my crotch coral, but I'm glad I did. And I'm glad I talked to my doctor about all of my sexual activities. And I asked my doctor if I was healthy enough for sexual activity. He told me that many men taking **Panacea** experience detachment of the genitals during intercourse, and I should contact him immediately if this happened to me. Then he told me **again** that with proper *diet and exercise* and **Panacea**, I could control the size and jaggedness of my crotch coral (in some cases).

Panacea is not for everyone.

Contact your physician immediately if you experience:

Vague feelings of unease, rapid snap-coiling of the penis, taste buds in the colon, giant eye-maggots, more boring thoughts, way too many legs, no more skin, a bird living in your larynx (sometimes called a larynx-bird), leaping dandruff, toes everywhere, donkey-laughing in your sleep, pooh on your elbow, weak stream, strong stream.

Consult your physician immediately if your sinuses become packed with ticks as this may be a sign of a more serious condition. If your tongue dries out and withers (a condition known as jerky-tongue), ask your physician about ways to control the urge to eat your tongue. Talk to your doctor soon on this one.

Women taking **Panacea** should anticipate experiencing all of these conditions, only more severely.

You're not too impressed with fancy slogans

You don't really care what others think you want to do

You've heard enough about new improved gadgets that somebody thinks you can't live without.

And when you shave you use

SEPTAQUA 7,000

Finally a razor with seven blades

Ernst Ernst Ernst & Ernst became the **world's largest and most powerful** law firm in the world by working only with claims against Juggernaut Pharmaceuticals.

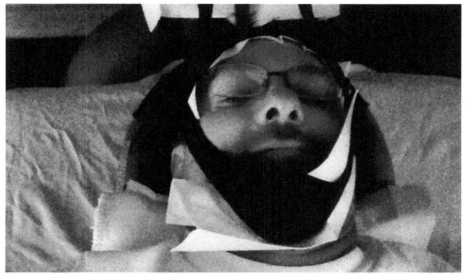

Actual client still undergoing treatment

Ernst Ernst Ernst & Ernst has brought financial relief to millions.

Now Ernst Ernst Ernst & Ernst and Juggernaut Pharmaceuticals are **teaming up** to bring you even better results. Now if you have a medical issue related to taking any Juggernaut Pharmaceutical medication you can simply go to Juggernaut online and **file your claim**, and while you're there, fill any of your Juggernaut prescriptions online.

FINALLY SOMEBODY GETS IT

1 (555)-ERNSTERNSTERNSTANDERNST

The law offices of
ERNST ERNST ERNST & ERNST

𝔗𝔥e 𝔐etro 𝔇ailp 𝔗imes 𝔊azette 𝔅ulgler

When you've got to know, you know where you've got to go

"...by the time you've figured it out, your eyes have been pecked out."

NOW YOU KNOW
WITH STU CRANSTENCE

Feff from Minnesota asks,
"Stu, where do mountain lions go in the winter?"
Stu Cranstence:
"Feff, no one knows where the mountain lions go in the winter, which is another thing that makes them so endangered. No one knows where they are, and by the time you've figured it out, your eyes have been pecked out.
In places like Iceland, it gets so cold that the mountain lions lose their beaks. Iceland is extremely cold - that's why it's on the North pole."

The Metro Daily Times Gazette Bugler has learned that local amateur scientist and lecturer, Stu Cranstence will be a passenger on the ***Princess Behemoth*** on its voyage to Mexico and Bermuda. He will be giving lectures on deck 27 each day at 4 pm. He has promised to bring some of his findings to share with what he refers to as the "ignorant public."

Passengers will also be able to fill as many international prescriptions for Simply More products and Juggernaut Pharmaceutical medications as they can safely carry.

SIMPLY MORE

The ultimate bulking agent

Founder Hugh Brown

Do you want to get more out of yourself?

*"Friends I created **Simply More**, the Ultimate Bulking Agent so that ordinary people like you and me could do something **extraordinary**. Today, the problem of **sub-satisfactory stool production** is being overcome by millions of **Simply More** users."*

Check out out all the latest formulas;
***Simply More** with Girth*
***Simply More** with Accelerator*
***Simply More** Ladies Formula*
***Simply More** for Dogs*
***Simply More** for Senior Dogs*

Isn't it nice to know that in the world of uncertainty, you can count on Simply More?

Some training recommended.
To get started just LOG ON.

WHAT DO I WANT?

SIMPLY MORE

Hey guys!

Check out our new catalog of possibilities
See pictures of our latest developments:

- Prehensile upgrade(hot seller)
- Loop shafts
- Multiple testicles

Also heavy-duty motorized carts that can be strapped on the front to solve your transport problems.

Call the **Male Adequacy Clinic** today.

Satisfied customer - L.L

Think of how bad you feel already, and think of how bad you'll feel if you get left **even further behind.**

The Male Adequacy Clinic

Chapter Five
Brought to you by the Flextrek Whipsnake – Sidewinder Edition

SO
THAT'S YOUR
BACKPACK
HUH?

You've had it for years and it's never let you down.

Your old backpack is good enough............. right?

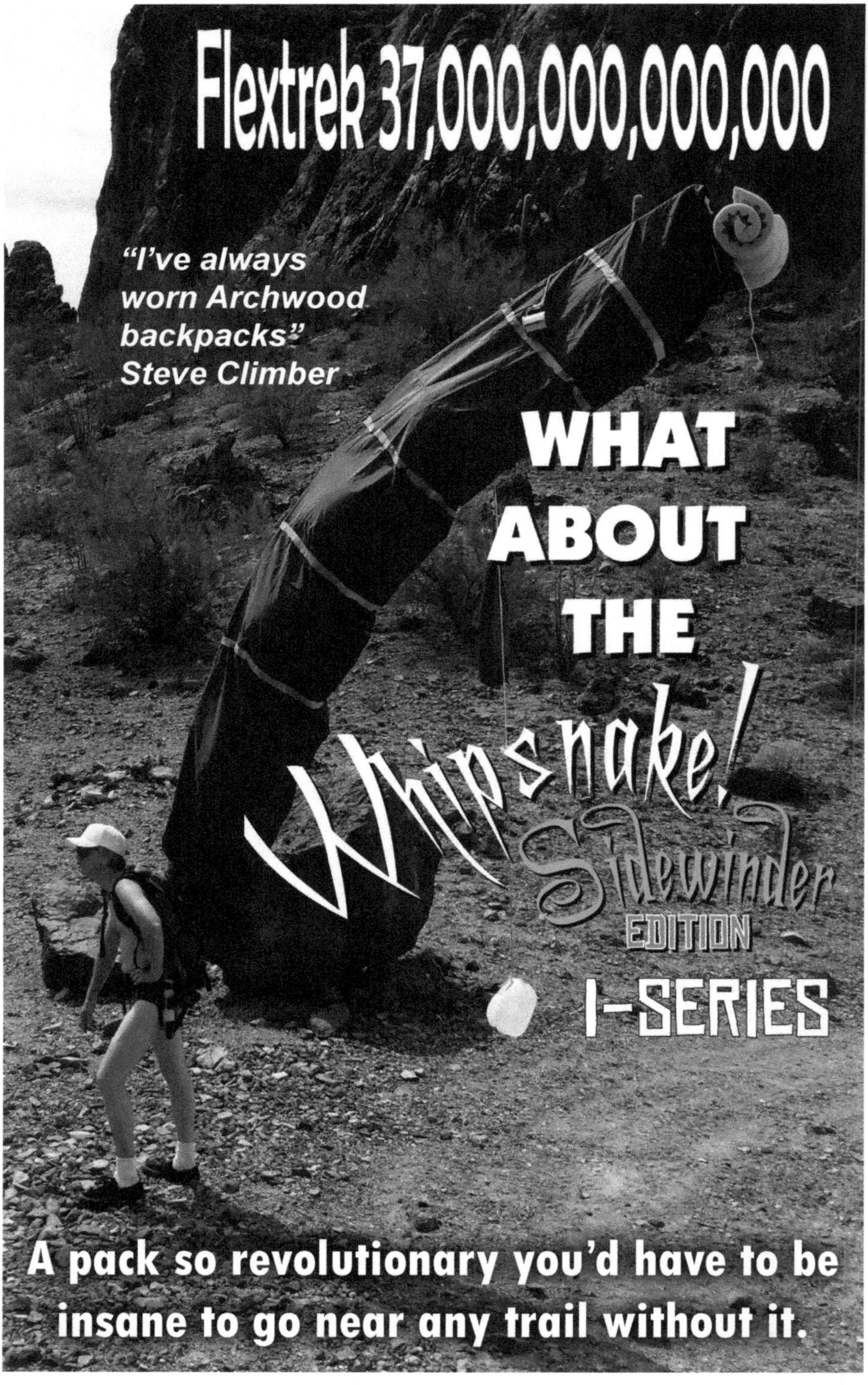
Flextrek 37,000,000,000,000
"I've always worn Archwood backpacks" Steve Climber
WHAT ABOUT THE
Whipsnake!
Sidewinder
EDITION
I-SERIES
A pack so revolutionary you'd have to be insane to go near any trail without it.

OUR MOST RESPONSIVE PACK YET!

SPACE AGE RESPONSO-FLEX CONSTRUCTION

YOU'RE SMART!

YOU'VE BEEN DOWN A TRAIL OR TWO

YOU KNOW WHAT GEAR YOU NEED

You don't let people tell you what to do and that's why you always buy Archwood!
You've seen fads come and go, that's why you always buy the latest Archwood backpack.

IT'S CALLED JUST BEING SMART

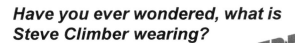

"I wear my **Whipsnake** and **Le Crevasse** in the harshest of terrain and the most demanding of environments. Sometimes the traction isn't always secure, and one's feet may fail to gain purchase, so it's good to know I can count on **Le Crevasse** and my **Flextrek 37,000,000,000,000 - Whipsnake edition** for maneuverability, durability and of course, comfort."
Steve Climber

GO
AHEAD
DEVASTATE
THE
ENVIRONMENT
HUMILIATE
THE
TERRAIN
YOU
DESERVE
IT!

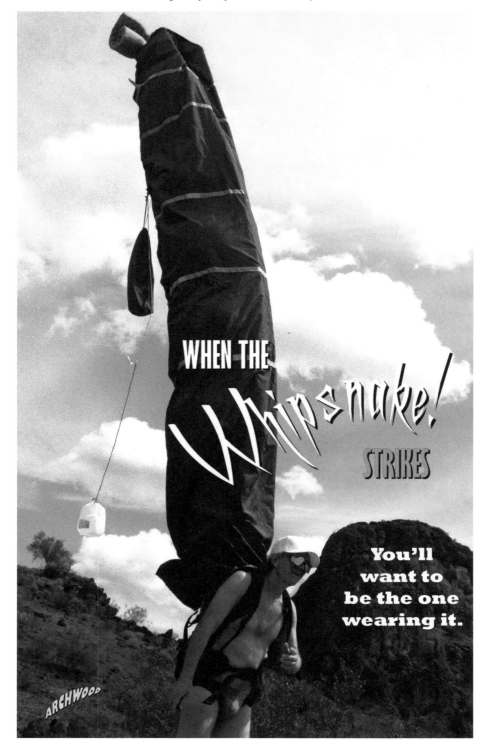

Skinflairtrynsol

Juggernaut pharmaceuticals

1 hour PLUS

maximum strenth

read all directions carefully.

Do not take if you have consumed alcohol within the last 90 days
Do not combine with drugs not made by Juggernaut Pharmaceuticals
Please feel free to combine with any and all of the Juggernaut medications
Do not take more than 72 doses in any 24 hour period
Ask your doctor if you are healthy enough to engage in sexual activity while taking Skinflairtrynsol
Tell your doctor about ALL your sexual activities
If you are taking Skinflairtrynsol with Myscleetra, ask your doctor about taking Stryreechlinstral

25 coated tablets
12,714mg each

DIRECTIONS:
TAKE ONE SKINFLAIRTRYNSOL TABLET AT EVEN INTERVALS SEVEN TIMES A DAY. THIS MEDICINE IS BELIEVED TO EASE YOUR CHRONIC DRY EAR(CDE) SYMPTOMS. TAKE 7 HOURS BEFORE OR 9 HOURS AFTER EATING. YOU SHOULD FEEL CONSIDERABLE MOISTURE IN YOUR INNER EAR WITHIN 7 DAYS OF STARTING THIS MEDICATION. DO NOT ABUSE THIS MEDICATION. DO NOT WASH DOWN THIS MEDICATION WITH ALCOHOL. OFF LABEL USES OF SKINFLAIRTRYNSOL SUCH AS COMBINING WITH TWO PANACEAS AND A SIX PACK OF CREN BEER(KNOWN ON COLLEGE CAMPUSES AS "THE KICKER")ARE NOT RECOMMENDED. DO NOT CONFUSE SKINFLAIRTRYNSOL WITH SKLINFLAIRTRYNSOL, CLINFLAIRTRINSOL, SKINLAIRFINTROL OR LINSKLAIRFINTOL AS THESE ARE VERY DIFFERENT MEDICATIONS. OVER USE OF SKINFLAIRTRYNSOL MAY WORSEN YOUR CONDITION. DO NOT UNDER ANY CIRCUMSTANCES STOP TAKING SKINFLAIRTRYNSOL AS THIS WILL RESULT IN CATATONIA.

SIDE EFFECTS MAY INCLUDE(BUT ARE NOT LIMITED TO):
VAGUE FEELINGS OF UNEASE (VFS), RAPID SNAP COILING OF THE PENIS (RSC), TASTE BUDS IN THE COLON (TBIMC), GIANT EYE MAGGOTS (GEM), SCALDING URINE, EXTREME WALL-EYE, WOMEN MAY FIND ONE BREAST WILL GROW VERY LARGE WHILE THE OTHER ONE WILL SHRINK DOWN TO PRACTICALLY NOTHING, MEN TAKING SKINFLAIRTRYNSOL SHOULD NOT HANDLE THEIR PRIVATE PARTS. SOME PEOPLE TAKING SKINFLAIRTRYNSOL WILL BECOME INCAPACITATED AND MAY REQUIRE EXTENDED HOSPITALIZATION. JUST BECAUSE A LOT OF CELEBRITIES TAKE SKINFLAIRTRYNSOL DOESN'T MEAN IT'S RIGHT FOR EVERYONE, ASK YOUR DOCTOR.

Skinflairtrynsol

Juggernaut Pharmaceuticals

ASK YOUR DOCTOR ABOUT ALL THE LATEST MEDICATIONS FROM JUGGERNAUT

WARNING!

THIS MEDICATION IS NOT APPROVED BY THE AMERICAN MEDICAL ASSOCIATION AND CARE SHOULD BE TAKEN WHEN USING THIS PRODUCT. THERE HAVE BEEN NUMEROUS REPORTS OF SERIOUS MEDICAL INJURIES AND DEFORMITIES RESULTING FROM THE USE OF THIS PRODUCT. JUGGERNAUT PHARMACEUTICALS IS NOT LICENSED IN THE UNITED STATES TO ADMINISTER MEDICATIONS OF ANY KIND THE ACTIVE INGREDIENTS IN THIS PRODUCT HAVE NOT BEEN TESTED BY THE FEDERAL DRUG ADMINISTRATION AND ARE NOT APPROVED FOR ANY TYPE OF USAGE WHATSOEVER. THE ACTIVE INGREDIENTS IN THIS PRODUCT ARE UNKNOWN TO THE STATE OF CALIFORNIA. THE OWNERS OF JUGGERNAUT PHARMACEUTICALS ARE WANTED BY FEDERAL, STATE AND LOCAL LAW ENFORCEMENT OFFICIALS FOR QUESTIONING ABOUT ILLEGAL PRACTICES. THIS PRODUCT HAS PROVEN TO BE HIGHLY ADDICTIVE. CARE SHOULD BE TAKEN. THIS PRODUCT SHOULD NOT BE TAKEN BY SENIORS, INFANTS, CHILDREN UNDER 15 YEARS OF AGE, ADULTS WHO HAVE HAD A PROBLEM WITH SUBSTANCE ABUSE AND ALL OTHERS.

PATIENTS TAKING **SKINFLAIRTRYNSOL** SHOULD NOT EAT ANY FOODS CONTAINING POLYBINUCLEAIC ACIDS. CONTRARY TO REPORTS IN THE MEDIA, **SKINFLAIRTRYNSOL** DOES **NOT** INCREASE SEXUAL APPETITE IN MARRIED WOMEN. YOUR DOCTOR WILL NEED TO BIOPSY YOUR LIVER AND SPLEEN TO DETERMINE IF **SKINFLAIRTRYNSOL** IS RIGHT FOR YOU. DO NOT COMBINE WITH **SKLINFLAIRTRYNISOL**. STILL HAVING **CDE** AFTER TAKING **SKINFLAIRTRYN-SOL** FOR 30 DAYS? TRY ADDING **PATHAGEN** AND **STRYREECHLINSTRAL** TO YOUR DAILY MEDICATIONS. ASK YOUR DR. IF YOU HAVE ANY PROBLEMS WITH A JUGGERNAUT PHARMACEUTICAL MEDICATION JUST CONTACT THE LAW OFFICES OF ERNST, ERSNT, ERNST, AND ERNST

IF YOU ARE TAKING SKLINFLAIRTRYNSOL WITH MYSCLEETRA, ASK YOUR DOCTOR ABOUT VYTRIOL
QUESTIONS? GO TO http://rhodesandrose.com/?page_id=456 WARNING: CONTAINS PHENYLALANINE

Still having CDE after 30 days on **Skinflairtrynsol**? Ask your doctor about adding **Pathajen** and **Stryreechlinstral** to your daily medications. Ask your doctor, and then get back to getting on with your life. Juggernaut: finding solutions to problems you didn't even know existed.

Chapter Six

Brought to you by Septaqua 7,000 – Finally a razor with seven blades.

Don't let your Chronic Dry Ear get in the way of your life. You may have CDE and not even know it.

People are asking, *is Chronic Dry Ear a real medical condition?* Well just ask the millions of people like you who are suffering from CDE and don't even know it. Finally there's a medication that fits YOUR needs thanks to Juggernaut Pharmaceuticals.

Skinflairtrynsol, along with proper *diet and exercise*, is thought to relieve the symptoms of CDE. Within just days you may feel considerable moisture pooling in your inner ear. Our new "7 times a day convenience" program makes taking **Skinflairtrynsol** easy. Don't let your CDE stop you from doing the things you really want to be doing.

Skinflairtrynsol is not for everyone.

Side effects may include:

Vague feelings of unease, rapid snap coiling of the penis(RSC), taste buds in the colon, giant eye-maggots, scalding urine, extreme wall-eye. Women taking **Skinflairtrynsol** may find one find one breast will grow very large while the other one will shrink down to practically nothing. Men taking **Skinflairtrynsol** should not handle their private parts.

Some people taking **Skinflairtrynsol** may become incapacitated and may require extended hospitalization. Over use may worsen your condition. Do not wash this medication down with alcohol. Your doctor may need to do a biopsy of your liver and spleen to determine if **Skinflairtrynsol** is right for you. Do not confuse **Skinflairtrynsol** with **Sklinflairtrynsol**, **Clinflairtrinsol**,or **Linsklairfintol**, as these are very different medications. Do not under any circumstances stop taking **Skinflairtrynsol** as this will result in catatonia. Just because lots of celebrities take **Skinflairtrynsol** doesn't mean it's right for everyone.

SIMPLY MORE
The ultimate bulking agent

Founder Hugh Brown

The bounds of what is possible no longer exist.

"Today, thanks to my mind boggling products, the problem of sub-satisfactory stool production is being overcome by **millions** of **Simply More** users. Thanks to **cutting-edge technology** and **innovation,** the bounds of what is possible no longer exist. Products like **Simply More** with Girth, **Simply More** with Accelerator for your busy schedule, **Simply More** Ladies Formula (the same **Simply More** quality ingredients in a lavender package), and thanks to a partnership with **Pet Chef** - products like **Simply More for Dogs** and **Simply More for Senior Dogs** are getting to the dogs that need them.
Simply More is the greatest product on earth. So ask yourself..."

WHAT DO I WANT?
SIMPLY MORE

(Training and a physicians prescription required by law.)

Not available in Utah and Mississippi.

The Metro Daily Times Gazette Bulgler

When you've got to know, you know where you've got to go

"Darwin (no one knows his last name) invented evolution nearly a hundred years ago."

NOW YOU KNOW
WITH STU CRANSTENCE

Darwin (no one knows his last name) invented evolution nearly a hundred years ago. One day he was walking in the forest and he saw five or six figures standing in a line. The first one was a monkey walking on all fours. The next one was standing a little straighter and by the time you got to the last one it was a man standing straight up! The disgusting thing is that the man was nude! You couldn't see his you-know-what because one leg was going forward, blocking the view. Even if you hold the page at an angle and look really close, you can't see anything.

Then Darwin went on to invent National Selection.

Darwin is also famous because he found the MISSING LINK. Scientists have been trying to find the MISSING LINK for over A HUNDRED YEARS. It's very hard to find because it's made out of CAMOUFLAGE. Darwin called it the 'Holy Grail' of science. He searched the globe for this elusive treasure which he knew would bring him fame and riches. He nearly found it in a cave but a GIANT BOULDER came rolling down at him and he barely escaped with his life. Even the huge bull whip he carried with him was useless against such a boulder.

*Then, in a very famous incident, he strapped a really ugly man to a table and turned the crank so the rope would pull the table up to the ceiling. Then lightning struck and as they say, **the rest is a mystery.***

Skinflairtrynsol

J uggernaut
pharmaceuticals

1 hour
maximum strenth
read all directions carefully.

PLUS

Do not take if you have consumed alcohol within the last 90 days
Do not combine with drugs not made by Juggernaut Pharmaceuticals
Please feel free to combine with any and all of the Juggernaut medications
Do not take more than 72 doses in any 24 hour period
Ask your doctor if you are healthy enough to engage in sexual activity while taking Skinflairtrynsol
Tell you doctor about ALL your sexual activities
If you are taking Skinflairtrynsol with Myscleetra, ask your doctor about taking Stryreechlinstral

25 coated tablets
12,714mg each

It has come to the attention of Juggernaut Pharmaceuticals that there may be some confusion regarding two of our ground-breaking medications. *We regret this confusion.* People have pointed out the similarity of the names and package designs of both of these medications. *We regret this similarity.* *DO NOT* confuse these two medications as they have drastically different reactions when combined with other Juggernaut medications. *DO NOT* take these two medications simultaneously. Study both of these packages carefully so that you will not accidentally take the wrong medication.

Sklinflairtrynsol

J uggernaut
pharmaceuticals

1 hour
maximum strenth
read all directions carefully.

PLUS

Do not take if you have consumed alcohol within the last 90 days
Do not combine with drugs not made by Juggernaut Pharmaceuticals
This is NOT Skinflairtrynsol! Do NOT combine Sklinflairtrynsol with Lethalis
Combining Sklinflairtrynsol with Skinflairtrynsol is very dangerous and should not be attempted
Do not take more than 72 doses in any 24 hour period
Ask your doctor if you are healthy enough to engage in sexual activity while taking Sklinflairtrynsol
Talk to your doctor about ALL your sexual activities
If you are taking Sklinflairtrynsol with Myscleetra, ask your doctor about taking Poisantin

25 coated tablets
12,714mg each

SIMPLY MORE
The ultimate bulking agent

Founder Hugh Brown

"I'd like to introduce you to my son, Bolus Brown who is here to represent the new face of Simply More. He's someone who understands that not only is Simply More the ultimate bulking agent, but that Simply More is the healthiest product on earth."

Bolus Brown

*"Thanks Dad. If you're like me, you don't have time to fool around with cheap imitations. You just want the best, and you want it now. **Just give me the ball and get the hell out of my way.** You also want to be on the cutting edge. That's why you'll want to know about **Simply More**'s new line, especially designed for the next generation... **Simply More with Worms.**"*

SIMPLY MORE WITH WORMS

Sure, it may not be for everybody...just winners.

WHAT DO I WANT?
SIMPLY MORE

(Possession of Simply More is a felony in some states)

For years Pet Chef has been the creator of flavors dogs can't resist, like Horse Chunks and Cheese and Grissel and Gravy with that extra meaty smell, so it's no surprise that they were the ones to finally come up with something so simple *your dog will never want to eat anything else.*

Can O' Ranch and *Can O' Blue* is *just what it says it is.* A whole can of Ranch or Blue Cheese dressing. *It's that simple.* The bottom line is your dog won't be able to think of anything else, except when they're going to get their next *Can O' Ranch* or *Can O' Blue* from Pet Chef. *End of story.*

All dogs love dressing!

Bolus Brown

"If you haven't tried the new Can O' Ranch or Can O' Blue from Pet Chef, what are you waiting for? I'm out of here."

𝕿𝕳𝖊 𝕸𝖊𝖙𝖗𝖔 𝕯𝖆𝖎𝖑𝖞 𝕿𝖎𝖒𝖊𝖘 𝕲𝖆𝖟𝖊𝖙𝖙𝖊 𝕭𝖚𝖑𝖌𝖑𝖊𝖗

When you've got to know, you know where you've got to go

STEG PRONGSTEN ATTACKED
BY KELP ON EVIL QUEEN BEACH

A photographer for the Metro Daily Times Gazette Bugler caught some dramatic photos of world class athlete Steg Prongsten being attacked by a species of white kelp on Evil Queen Beach. The kelp became very aggressive after Prongsten had completed several runs up and down the deserted beach. There have been no reports of kelp attacks on Evil Queen Beach for several decades. Kelp bites can be very dangerous as they often leave a stinger inside the victim that has to be carefully removed with pliers. Prongsten is recovering in a local hospital.

Juggernaut Pharmaceuticals strives to give you answers to the problems you haven't even developed yet - *but we can't solve your problems unless you partner with us*. As a partner it's **very important** that you ask your doctor about ALL of the medications that Juggernaut advertises. If you haven't asked your doctor about Stryreechlinstral, Lethalis, Poisantin, Pandemical, Panacea, Skinflairtrynsol, or Sklinflairtryinsol yet, ask them TODAY.

And then you should ask yourself why you haven't already asked your doctor about these medications.

As a partner in our "Circle of Healing" we ask you to be an active member and be involved in your own health.

The most important thing you can do for Juggernaut Pharmaceuticals is to ASK YOUR DOCTOR about ALL of our medications. We want YOU to be in control of your health.

If your doctor doesn't want to prescribe any or all of our medications to you, we encourage you to tell us who your doctor is so that we can put that doctor on our "Circle of Health" watch-list. That doctor will then no longer receive free merchandise or cruise tickets. In this way, we can encourage doctors to prescribe more and more, and get our ground breaking medications to the people that want and need them.

Thank you.

Rootsin Toobers

Juggernaut
Pharmaceuticals

Seven blades, you gotta be kidding me. It's way too much, right?

I mean, c'mon. It's way more than I need, right?

WRONG!

When you shave you use
SEPTAQUA 7,000
Finally a razor with seven blades

GOT TOO MUCH FAT?

Tune in weekday mornings at 3:30 as Hundus
and Furundus show you the proper technique
for the classic jumping jack exercise.

Your fat doesn't stand a chance.
Watch in amazement as they show off some
unbelievable exercises and martial arts moves.
Let these two fitness gurus show you how to lose the fat the old
fashioned way, **one pound at a time!**
Watch their unconventional form and technique.
Get up early with Hundus and Furundus and

start losing it!

**Look for the upcoming episode featuring Hundus
demonstrating his incredible gas regimen! He combines
exercise with a diet containing large amounts of
kidney beans, dried fruit, caramelized onions, and hard
boiled eggs. You'll be winded too after this workout!**

The Metro Daily Times Gazette Bulgler

When you've got to know, you know where you've got to go

NOW YOU KNOW
WITH STU CRANSTENCE

Question for Stu Cranstence from Old Pappy:
"Last night I had a large can of Dinty Moore stew for supper along with two packs of jalapeño Slim Jims. I felt fine. At bed time I took my normal dose of Stryreechlinstral and my coumadin. I was awakened in the middle of the night to have a very disturbing bowel movement. Should I take an additional dose of Lethalis to help me with this problem?"

OLD PAPPY

Stu Cranstence:
"Old pappy? I haven't heard from you since…well you know. Anyway, I don't know why people want to ask me about their disgusting problems. Meanwhile, you probably don't know about my findings, like Bonesticks. Bonesticks are bones that are so old that they've turned into sticks that are bones, but actually they're sticks. That's why they're called Stickbones.

*As far as your question, Old Pappy. Just don't get the medicines mixed up, but if you do, take extra, just to make sure. You can try not to drink alcohol with them if you want. I don't know if it's Pandemical or Myscleetra - one of them clears up most of the problems. The Skinflairtrynsol doesn't seem to work anymore, but I've got a lot of them. My weak stream gets real strong with one of them, I think it's Poisantin. I say, when in doubt, take the Stryreechlinstral. It's been around over a year now, so it's got a track record. The main thing is **ask you doctor about the new ones! How's he going to give them to you if you don't ask for them?"***

"A bonestick is bone that's so old it's turned into a stick, but actually it's a bone," Stu Cranstence

𝕿𝖍𝖊 𝕸𝖊𝖙𝖗𝖔 𝕯𝖆𝖎𝖑𝖞 𝕿𝖎𝖒𝖊𝖘 𝕲𝖆𝖟𝖊𝖙𝖙𝖊 𝕭𝖚𝖑𝖌𝖑𝖊𝖗

When you've got to know, you know where you've got to go

Medical Minute question for Dr. Soily Kruebens.

Mr. S. writes,

Hello Doctor. I've been using Simply More - the ultimate bulking agent - for a few months. I am not questioning the results. I mean this stuff is unbelievable. I'm wondering if any insurance companies cover the cost of the products?

Dr. Soily Kruebens;

*Amazingly, no insurance company will cover the cost of **Simply More**, except for Insure-All which does offer some coverage depending on what policy you have. I don't want to get on a soapbox here, but sometimes I wonder why is it that insurance companies won't cover bulking agent? Now, thanks to Insure-All, I think we're coming around on that one.*

*Did you know that in most of the world people cannot afford **Simply More** products? Not even the low priced Basic Formula Program! It doesn't have to be that way. In an exciting new partnership with Juggernaut Pharmaceuticals, **Simply More** hopes to bring the hope of **Simply More** to the rest of the world.*

WHAT DO I WANT?
SIMPLY MORE

(Contact Simply More for information on our personal trainer program.)

I'm busy making my dreams come true.

MYSCLEETRA
Juggernaut
Pharmaceuticals

"When I think back on how large and aggressive the bird in my larynx had become, I'm glad that I asked my doctor about Myscleetra."

When the aggressiveness of my larynx bird began to get in between me and my dreams, I knew it was time to ask my doctor about **Myscleetra**. I knew I needed to take control of the size and aggressiveness of the bird living in my larynx (or larynx-bird), that developed as a result of taking **Panacea**. Not everyone who takes **Panace**a will develop a bird in their larynx, (or larynx-bird)...

I did.

So I asked my doctor about **Myscleetra**, and he said that with proper *diet and exercise* and **Myscleetra**, I'd be the one in control of the size and aggressiveness of the bird in my larynx, or larynx-bird. *Now it's my larynx-bird.*

Myscleetra is not for everyone.

Contact your physician if you experience:

Vague feelings of unease, rapid snap-coiling of the penis, taste buds in the colon, giant eye-maggots, repeated lightning strikes to the face, pus squirting out of your eyes, ears, naval, and shoulders, freeway sleep-walking, singing testicles, singing testicles in the nasal passage, nasal passages in the testicles, all your hairs become teeth, a wart that really does worry, eels migrating through your intestines, eels spawning in your pancreas, confessing to crimes you did not commit, inability to hit clutch free-throws, severe brand loyalty.

Contact your physician if your body decomposes as this may be a sign of a more serious condition. Women taking **Myscleetra** should expect to give birth to a full-grown narwhal every three to four months. If you're over fifty and taking **Myscleetra**, you should expect to die immediately. If you're taking **Myscleetra**, don't use a weed whacker. Contact your physician if you take a dump on the grocery checkout conveyor belt as this is often an incurable behavior disorder.

Isn't
it good
to know
You can
count on
Steve Climber?
He
comes
through
every time

Everybody
loves
Steve Climber
Because
he's
climbing
all
around

Ernst Ernst Ernst & Ernst & Juggernaut: The Dream Team

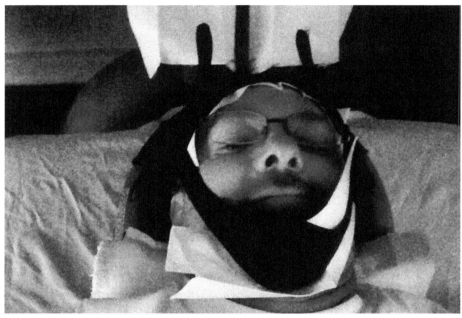

Actual client undergoing ongoing treatment

Ever since Ernst Ernst Ernst & Ernst and Juggernaut Pharmaceuticals have teamed up, it's so easy to file a claim **and** fill your prescriptions. Just come on down. Our new offices occupy the entire 78th floor of Juggernaut Pharmaceuticals Tower. We will help you negotiate the local laws and restrictions and get you the international prescription you need - and then get you started on a lawsuit.

FINALLY SOMEBODY GETS IT

1 (555)-ERNSTERNSTERNSTANDERNST

The law offices of
ERNST ERNST ERNST & ERNST

Chapter Seven
Brought to you by Pet Chef

The Metro Daily Times Gazette Bulgler
When you've got to know, you know where you've got to go

HUGH BROWN BUILDS WORLD'S TALLEST CRUISE SHIP

Simply More founder Hugh Brown has amassed an incredible fortune selling his controversial product. He has used part that new-found wealth to buy an existing cruise ship, cut off the top, add 10 additional decks, and then put the top back on, creating a commanding vessel that was re-named the Princess Behemoth. The ship now has a passenger capacity of 16,788, plus 3,267 crew members, making it the largest cruise ship in the world.

As part of the retrofit, Brown had all of the plumbing and sewage facilities upgraded to accommodate the anticipated increase in effluent caused by cruise going Simply More enthusiasts. Now each cabin comes with a powerful jet flush toilet especially designed to handle the huge amount of output that is expected.

A maritime architect (who declined to be identified) called the project to add that many decks to an existing vessel "ill-advised" and warned of instability in extreme weather conditions caused by the high profile. Environmental experts have also questioned the use of high pressure nozzles to spray all of the effluent out of the stern in an effort to increase speed and save fuel.

The cruise is scheduled to sail to Mexico and Bermuda (weather permitting).

𝕿𝖍𝖊 𝕸𝖊𝖙𝖗𝖔 𝕯𝖆𝖎𝖑𝖞 𝕿𝖎𝖒𝖊𝖘 𝕲𝖆𝖟𝖊𝖙𝖙𝖊 𝕭𝖚𝖑𝖌𝖑𝖊𝖗

When you've got to know, you know where you've got to go

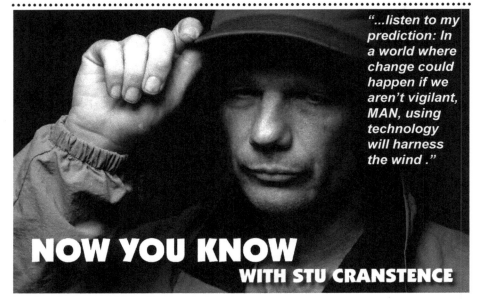

"...listen to my prediction: In a world where change could happen if we aren't vigilant, MAN, using technology will harness the wind ."

NOW YOU KNOW
WITH STU CRANSTENCE

Question for Stu Cranstence from Alan Rose:
"Hi Stu. My name is Dr. Alan Rose. I currently work at the University of California at Davis. I'm a plant molecular biologist. I got my PhD at Princeton University. I have a question for you. During the elongation phase of transcription, is the carboxy terminal domain of RNA polymerase II phosphorylated on serine 5 or serine 2?"

Stu Cranstence:
"Well in case you're wondering where I am right now, I'm out in the field, within the perimeter. I'm in an AREA. AREAS are part of the environment, and I'm within the perimeter. As far as answering your question - ALAN - part of the joy of being out in the field where there aren't people, is knowing that I won't have to talk to people like you who want to question my FINDINGS - even though I already put them in boxes and labeled them and gave them to my brother Ron who had them verified by a real scientist, who I haven't even met because I was busy, but he said that the ancient pottery that I found was DEFINITIVE and CATEGORIZED as DROPPINGS. They're all at my brother Ron's who is probably verifying them. So as far as ALAN is concerned, keep up your efforts. If you're interested in the future of science, listen to my prediction: In a world where change could happen if we aren't vigilant, MAN, using technology, will harness the wind - as far fetched as that sounds - to use the power of the wind to create energy - GASOLINE - all within our children's lifetime. That's called science, ALAN!"

The Holiday Caravan Cruises
to Mexico, Bermuda and beyond

Princess Behemoth

We've got great news. We are going to drastically reduce the ticket price on this cruise. Are you ready for this? ***$29.95!!***

For less than $30 you get **10** days and nights of absolute tropical luxury.

How do we do this? First of all, this ship is the biggest in the world, and you will *not believe* how many people we can fit on this boat. But secondly, through great fortune on one of our recent cruises, we encountered a remote island and a group of people there who had been cut off from their traditional trading ties and because of the resulting disease and poverty found themselves in a state of complete desperation. *And there's thousands of them.* And they will work for practically nothing! What a delight to be around people who will do anything for you. And you don't even have to tip them! They're happy just to be alive!

$29.95!! It seems like nothing to you and me, but to our crew, it's a **fortune,** so they treat you like ***royalty***. You don't even have to treat them well at all!

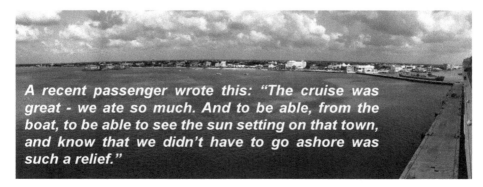

A recent passenger wrote this: "The cruise was great - we ate so much. And to be able, from the boat, to be able to see the sun setting on that town, and know that we didn't have to go ashore was such a relief."

SIMPLY MORE

The ultimate bulking agent

Founder Hugh Brown

"I remember being lied to as a child. Being told there was nothing I could do about my personal output. My parents didn't even encourage me in my desire to produce more, MUCH more stool. In contrast, here is my son to tell you about our newest breakthrough formulas!"

Bolus Brown

*"Hey, I don't really have time hear about your old yesterday's news. But if you want to give me what's hot now, **thanks**, I'll take it...**ALL**, and **catch you in the rearview mirror**. Listen up. Simply More's put together a **new combo formula** for those of us who aren't about to be content with anything but the **ultimate**:*
*Simply More with Girth and Simply More with Worms have been combined into one - **Simply More with Girth with Worms with Girth.***
End of story."

SIMPLY MORE WITH GIRTH WITH WORMS WITH GIRTH

That's a real mouthful!

WHAT DO I WANT?

SIMPLY MORE

(Simply More is no longer available in some states)

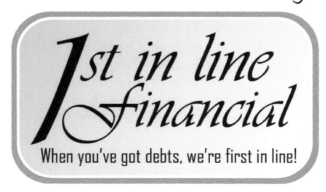

The Metro Daily Times Gazette Bulgler

When you've got to know, you know where you've got to go

AREA MAN HAS PLAQUE REMOVED

Area man, Stu Cranstence, recently had a ribbon-cutting ceremony to dedicate a plaque that he had made and installed at an overlook on the highway. Within hours local transportation officials had removed the plaque as they claim it was an unauthorized installation and would not comment on the plaque's content or current location.

The plaque read as follows:

"What you are looking at is a picture of me - Stu Cranstence.
But if you look up over this picture of me,
way off in the distance, you will see a lake!
Damn Lake.
How did Damn Lake get there?
No one knows - it's too steep and crumbly to get down there.
Damn Lake is in an AREA. This AREA is over a hundred years old!
It was invented by the ANCIENT EGYPTIANS.
No one spoke English back then - they only spoke CHINESE.
Some people say, 'Oh, we're running out of water.'
That is why I insist that we build more damns.
We should make a damn in every canyon and on top of every mountain.
First we build the damns then sit back and watch the water come squirting out.
Problem solved!
Now you know."
Stu Cranstence - President of Stu Cranstence's Institutes of the Sciences

WHAT IS STEVE CLIMBER WEARING?

The FRENCH WEDGE

The French Wedge is made of a revolutionary fabric that binds your hair, perspiration and sloughed off skin cells to the fabric of the Wedge, actually making it stronger with every step.

Don't get caught looking like a fool on the trail. Thanks to the good people at Archwood, anyone can look like Steve Climber. And remember, because it's a French Wedge, it...

NEVER NEEDS WASHING!

It just keeps getting stronger!

Hey guys!

Did you know that male enhancement surgery has become so popular and effective that you'd have to be a fool not to want one - **or maybe more?** At the Male Adequacy Clinic multiples are our fastest growing area. Think of how bad you feel already, and think of how bad you'll feel if you get left **even further behind.**
The Male Adequacy Clinic has received many of this years industry awards, including the fastest service, shortest stay award. And yes, you can get yours with a hoof!

Satisfied customer - J.F.

There's no stopping us now!

The Male Adequacy Clinic

The Metro Daily Times Gazette Bulgler

When you've got to know, you know where you've got to go

"Avalanche is an ancient Chinese word. It means avalanche."

NOW YOU KNOW
WITH STU CRANSTENCE

Question from Taco:
"What are avalanches, and can terrorists use them against us to take our freedoms?"
Stu Cranstence:
*"Avalanches are **features of the environment**. They were invented over a hundred years ago. Back then nobody spoke English, they only spoke Chinese. In fact, avalanche is an ancient Chinese word. It means **avalanche**. When an avalanche erupts, hot lava - heated to over a hundred degrees - comes pouring out the top.*

Taco

*This is caused, when deep beneath the earth, sodium bicarbonate - or baking soda - comes in contact with vinegar from the earth's core. Terrorists can use these techniques to take our freedoms. That is why terrorists should not be allowed to travel to our country. They should take their vacations elsewhere. There are many resorts in other countries for terrorists to spend their holidays and vacations. **These countries already have avalanches, so it doesn't matter if they're destroyed.**"*

(The opinions in this column are Stu Cranstence's alone and are not necessarily the opinion of The Metro Daily Times Gazette Bugler.)

Always talk to your doctor about the detachment of your genitals.

Thanks Juggernaut!

"Now, thanks to Pathagen, I'm the one that's in control of my genitals"

When my genitals became detached during intercourse, I knew it was time to talk to my doctor about **Pathagen**. My doctor told me that the detachment of my genitals was a result of taking **Panacea** to control the size and the jaggedness of the crotch coral that I developed as a result of taking **Pandemical** for the giant eye-maggots which were caused by **Poisantin** which I take to control the size and sensitivity of the taste buds in my colon that began emerging after I started taking **Lethalis** which put me in charge of my rapid snap-coiling penis that I first noticed after I started taking **Stryreechlinstral** to help me deal with my vague feelings of unease.

Not everyone who takes **Panacea** will experience detachment of the genitals during intercourse...

I did.

So I asked my doctor about **Pathagen**, and he told me that with proper *diet and exercise* and **Pathagen** I would be the one in control of the detachment of my genitals.

Always talk to your doctor during intercourse if you experience detachment of your genitals during intercourse. If you're taking **Pathagen** with **Myscleetra**, ask your doctor about taking **Skinflairtrynsol**.

Once you start taking Pathagen, don't stop.

SIMPLY MORE
The ultimate bulking agent

Do you walk out of the bathroom and ask yourself – is that all there is?

Founder Hugh Brown

"Why be satisfied with the ordinary output that so many people seem to just accept? Don't you deserve more? Of course you do!

Thanks to Simply More - the ultimate bulking agent, you can start producing quantities that are going to ***blow you away!"***

Don't take our word for it.

Just ask **Simply More** user **Bret B.**

"My friends said I was crazy when I told the m about the amount of stool I wanted to produce. But after only a few weeks on the Simply More products, I really showed them. Hey guys! Who's crazy now?"

To find out more LOG ON When you see what we offer on our website, you'll really be ready to download.

WHAT DO I WANT?
SIMPLY MORE

(Simply More is no longer sold in stores. Call our new offshore office. ORDER NOW. Time may be running out.)

The Metro Daily Times Gazette Bugler

When you've got to know, you know where you've got to go

PRONGSTEN BITTEN IN FACE

A photographer for the Metro Daily Times Gazette Bugler caught some more dramatic photos of world-class athlete Steg Prongsten being attacked by a species of white kelp on Evil Queen Beach. The kelp have became very aggressive ever since Steg Prongsten started training in the area. He has been bitten repeatedly, but this has not deterred him from his training regimen.

Scientists are baffled as to why the kelp have been attacking Prongsten in particular. Locals hold the opinion that his training has awoken the kelp queen from a 10,000 year slumber and that his training apparel has offended her deeply.

When asked if he was concerned about being attacked again by kelp Prongsten stated, "I'm a world-class athlete. I travel the globe looking for the ultimate settings to train and test the limits of human fitness. Do really think I'm going to be afraid of some damn seaweed? If you don't mind, I've got some actual training to do."

Shortly after he made this statement he was struck in the face by a particularly aggressive specimen of white kelp. Legend has it that the white kelp have no soul, although this could not be confirmed by marine biologists.

If you're going to get too far into debt, we want you to do it with us.

We've got an exciting announcement. First in Line Financial is beginning a mass mailing campaign you'll want to know about. We're sending out money! That's right. In the next few days, most residents in the area will receive a check for **$500.** If you choose to use that money, you will instantly become part of the First in Line Financial family. By simply depositing your check, First in Line Financial collection officers, or Partners in Trust, will immediately contact you to let you know how you can participate in the growth of First in Line Financial.
Vacations! Cars! Clothes!
They're all on their way. So keep an eye on that mailbox - unless of course you don't want any money!

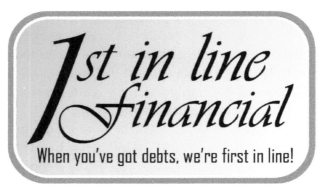

1st in line financial

When you've got debts, we're first in line!

There's nothing more important in life than Juggernaut Pharmaceuticals.

Consumer Magazine reports that Juggernaut keeps people alive 12% longer than other pharmaceutical companies. That's better for us here at Juggernaut, too. We plan on having you around to enjoy Juggernaut products year after year!

At Juggernaut we're busy doing just one thing, saving all life on earth.

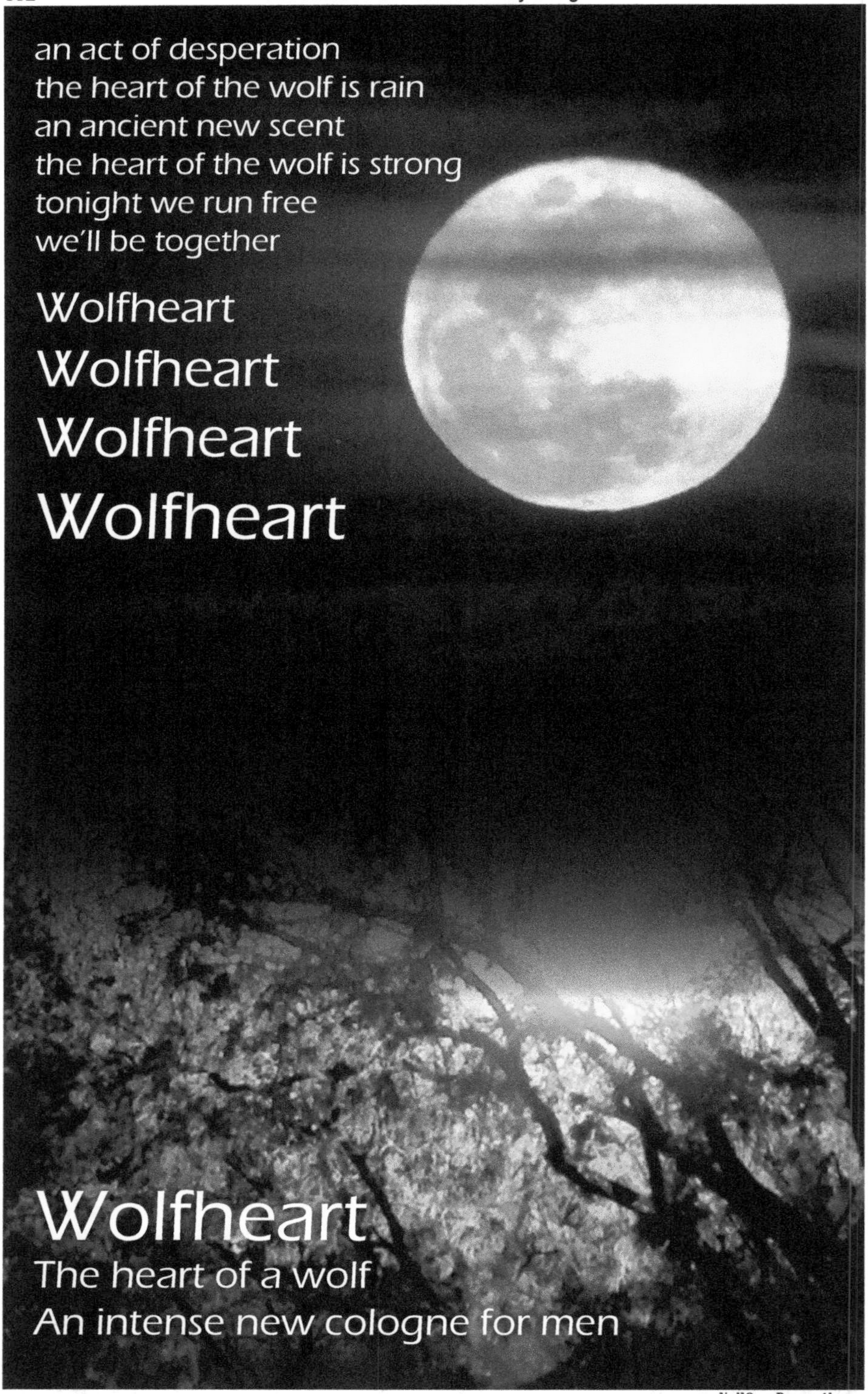
an act of desperation
the heart of the wolf is rain
an ancient new scent
the heart of the wolf is strong
tonight we run free
we'll be together
Wolfheart
Wolfheart
Wolfheart
Wolfheart
Wolfheart
The heart of a wolf
An intense new cologne for men

NailGun Promotions

What do you call it when you get more than you expected? I call it about time.

SIMPLY MORE
The ultimate bulking agent

Just remember that Simply More is the healthiest product on earth.

Founder Hugh Brown

"Years ago when I create the Simply More formula, all I wanted to do was substantially increase the amount of stool I was producing. People asked me, *'Hugh, why in God's name would you want to do something like that?'* Well those people had no idea that my simple dream would someday become the dream of the entire world. With the aid of cutting edge technology like GPS satellite systems, Simply More is bringing its formula for success to even the most remote places on earth - even places as remote as the Venezuelan rain forest.

Remember that whenever you hear anything negative about Simply More or something that calls into question the safety of Simply More, just remember that Simply More is the healthiest product on earth."

WHAT DO I WANT?
SIMPLY MORE

(Simply More is no longer available)

Chapter Eight

Brought to you by the Male Adequacy Clinic

𝕮𝖍𝖊 𝕸𝖊𝖙𝖗𝖔 𝕯𝖆𝖎𝖑𝖞 𝕿𝖎𝖒𝖊𝖘 𝕲𝖆𝖟𝖊𝖙𝖙𝖊 𝕭𝖚𝖑𝖌𝖑𝖊𝖗

When you've got to know, you know where you've got to go

AREA MAN PUBLISHES BOOK

Local amateur scientist Stu Cranstence has published his first book titled, MY Findings. One reviewer describes it as "a book that reshapes expectations about literacy and science in the 21st century." Another writes, "Stu is utterly incredible. His methods and conclusions are unlike those of any trained scientist. You would be unbelievably lucky to have Stu make a finding of any significance on your land."

There are 78 photographs to illustrate his findings in this slim volume published by Hardy Perennial Press. It sells for $12.95 and is available on Amazon.com Ten chapters give readers information about Types of Rocks, Fast Growing Mushrooms, and Bonesticks among many other topics.

MY Findings
by Stu Cranstence

From the back cover:

The findings of Stu Cranstence have, for years, filled countless cardboard boxes, trash cans and an aluminum shed in the back yard of his brother, Ron. These findings have been rescued from the ravages of time, mildew and Ron's shed and are collected here for the first time. This is the first volume in a series that will reveal and collect the depth and breadth of Cranstence's findings on a wide range of subjects from natural history to ancient cultures and modern scientific misconceptions.

This is more than merely a scientific volume, this book is also a look inside the mind of a man who sees the world as "my own large area. A huge display case full of MY ideas, MY discoveries...MY findings."

Hey guys!

How long has it been since your last male enhancement procedure?

We're all busy with our hectic lives. Sometimes we forget. We understand this, so that's why we send you a reminder when you're due for your next update procedure.

Just think of how bad you feel already, and how bad you'll feel if you get left even further behind.

Satisfied customer - S.C.

There's no stopping us now!

The Male Adequacy Clinic

Holiday Caravan Cruises to Mexico, Bermuda and beyond

Princess Behemoth

"This trip to Mexico and Bermuda is going to be dynamite!"

Founder Hugh Brown

"You've heard about the Simply More Travel Package Holiday Caravan Cruise to Mexico and Bermuda, and now you want to join in the fun.
They're filling up fast. On these trips you can get as many years worth of Simply More as you like, and an international prescription for ALL Simply More products."

"Dad, don't forget about Simply More with Worms."

"Thanks Bolus! The young people of today, you've got to admire their energy, and now you can also admire their worms. Simply More with Worms and all of the other terrific formulas will be available for purchase on this cruise. "

(The department of Homeland Security has announced that the Simply More Travel Package Holiday Caravan Cruise on the Princess Behemoth has been placed on hold, Homeland Security representatives will be present to answer question about Simply More and its availability.)

SIMPLY MORE

The ultimate bulking agent

Friends, it IS possible to produce more stool.

Founder Hugh Brown

"When people say to me, Hugh, what about all the problems in this world? Failing schools, overcrowded prisons, the slow march of global ecological degradation, war and the exploding world poverty? I say there's only one answer. Simply More. Why? Because Simply More is the ultimate bulking agent."

Simply More has highly skilled certified trainers standing by to assist our customers in every way possible (at no immediate cost). They will come to your home and do a hands-on assessment of what you're doing and the handling capacity of your facilities and make recommendations about any plumbing upgrades. Trainers are an essential part of our program, especially now with the increasing reports of abuse of our products.

Here's Certified Simply More trainer Ann Thusiast!

"As a Simply More trainer, I want to see what you can do...but do it right!"

WHAT DO I WANT?

SIMPLY MORE

(Simply More continues to be unavailable. Public demonstrations, no matter how large and violent, will not change Simply More's status.)

Your dog is more than just a pet. Your dog is part of the family.

In an exciting new collaboration, Pet Chef and Juggernaut Pharmaceuticals have teamed up to give your dog exactly what it needs. Now all of our classic flavors can come infused with Stryreechlinstral to help your dog with its vague feelings of unease.

Watch your the dog food aisle for more ground-breaking formulas.

Your dog is crazy...for Pet Chef

The Metro Daily Times Gazette Bulgler

When you've got to know, you know where you've got to go

HUGH BROWN ARRESTED

Hugh Brown, the eccentric billionaire founder of Simply More - the ultimate bulking agent, has been taken into custody in an operation run in cooperation with officials from the Drug Enforcement Agency, the Department of Homeland Security, the Environmental Protection Agency, the Centers for Disease Control and Prevention, the Department of Health and Human Services, the Food and Drug Administration and other federal, state and local law enforcement agents.

There is no word yet on what if any criminal charges have been filed against Brown. A spokesperson from Simply More put out a press release saying "despite rumors that the Simply More Travel Package Holiday Caravan Cruise has been put on hold, we are still scheduled to sail." Simply More has come under increasing scrutiny as its popularity has increased. Concerns have been raised about its health effects and impact on the environment.

Simply More and Brown are also the subjects of a number of civil lawsuits brought by municipal sewage treatment facilities and the owners of a number of high rise buildings. One worker at a treatment plant said off the record that they are being "overrun" and that you could "practically walk across the primary sedimentation tank" and that the sludge digestion tank is a "goner."

Several owners of high rise buildings with a large percentage of Simply More users have complained that their vertical sewer drain pipes are over capacity and have to be regularly bored out at considerable cost.

A spokesperson from the law firm of Ernst Ernst Ernst & Ernst who are representing Brown would not comment as they are also representing the tenants and building owners who are suing Brown.

SIMPLY MORE
The ultimate bulking agent

Friends, I won't be in jail forever.

Founder Hugh Brown

"Friends, if you're not growing, you're dying. Simply More is not dying. Simply More is the ultimate bulking agent, and the answer to those who ask a simple question - how can I produce more stool? Before I introduced my Simply More products, most people were satisfied to produce the normal everyday kind of output that had actually become an accepted way of living, but Simply More has changed all that. What once seemed out of any reasonable realm of possibility is now becoming the expectation of an entire planet.

Friends, *I won't be in jail forever.* When I come out I promise to reveal new exciting formulas that will capture your imagination in a way that would make our ancestors shake their heads in bewilderment."

WHAT DO I WANT?
SIMPLY MORE

(Pending legislation regulating the sale, purchase and possession of Simply More will be put to a final vote this Saturday)

In a world where animal shelters are full of unwanted pets, isn't it time your dog explored the possibilities of male enhancement surgery?

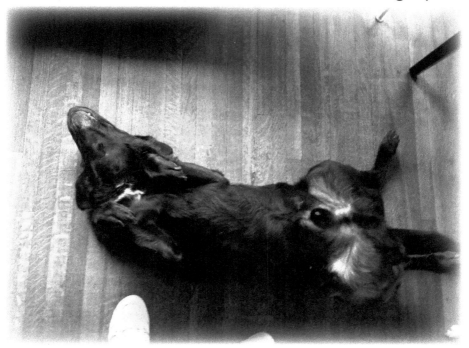

We think so too.

𝕿𝕳𝖊 𝕸𝖊𝖙𝖗𝖔 𝕯𝖆𝖎𝖑𝖞 𝕿𝖎𝖒𝖊𝖘 𝕲𝖆𝖟𝖊𝖙𝖙𝖊 𝕭𝖚𝖑𝖌𝖑𝖊𝖗

When you've got to know, you know where you've got to go

PRINCESS BEHEMOTH TO SAIL THIS SATURDAY!

The Simply More Travel Package Holiday Caravan Cruise to Mexico and Bermuda aboard the Princess Behemoth is scheduled to sail this Saturday, regardless of whether Simply More founder Hugh Brown is still in jail or not.

Due to ongoing legal battles with Federal, State and local officials, Simply More has decided to load its entire inventory of Simply More into the hold of the enormous ship. Forklifts have been loading pallet after pallet 24 hours a day in preparation for the voyage.

The Metro Daily Times Gazette Bugler has learned that Juggernaut Pharmaceuticals has also begun loading its entire North American inventory onto the ship as they battle similar regulatory issues. The Drug Enforcement Agency has recently begun the process of reclassifying all of Juggernaut's products as Schedule 1 controlled substances for having a high potential for abuse. A spokesperson said that in light of ongoing legal entanglements, Juggernaut felt it prudent to move all operations and inventory offshore until further notice.

It's unclear how much tonnage the Princess Behemoth is rated to carry since its redesign. The ship has settled noticeably lower in the water as more and more pallets are loaded on board.

Does your septic tank look like this because of Simply More?

Actual client's septic tank

If so, you may be eligible for financial compensation.

$$$$$$$$$$$$$

Contact the law offices of Ernst Ernst Ernst & Ernst immediately for information that will get you the help you deserve. All of our clients are people like you who are seeking financial relief to pay for the astronomical plumbing debt that is typical for Simply More customers.

CALL NOW!

1 (555)-ERNSTERNSTERNSTANDERNST

The law offices of

ERNST ERNST ERNST & ERNST

The Metro Daily Times Gazette Bulgler

AREA MAN ARRIVES AT THE PRINCESS BEHEMOTH

Local author Stu Cranstence was seen on his way to the dock to join the Simply More Travel Package Holiday Caravan Cruise to Mexico and Bermuda aboard the Princess Behemoth. His vehicle was loaded down with what he called "my findings."

Cranstence is claiming that he will be making "significant findings" while on the cruise, although it is not clear how he will be doing that seeing that the ship is not scheduled to be docking at any ports, but will be staying in international waters for the duration of the cruise. Cranstence is known for making most of his findings within what he calls 'the perimeter' which appears from his videos to be a small circle of land around his campsite.

Cranstence is also a spokesperson for Juggernaut Pharmaceuticals and will be available on board to answers any questions passengers may have about the ins and outs of being a Juggernaut medications user. He has extensive experience with all of Juggernaut's medications and can give tips and tricks to get the most out of them.

SIMPLY MORE
The ultimate bulking agent

Don't you worry about me, dear friends

Founder Hugh Brown

"Friends, this is Hugh Brown, from the belly of the beast, for Simply More the ultimate bulking agent.

Don't you worry about me, dear friends, my new circumstances are simply a new opportunity - an opportunity to dream - of new ways, of new days, when Simply More will be the only way of life worth living.

Friends, if you want to do something for Hugh brown, then after you've bought all the Simply More products you possibly can - products that have become the dream of an entire world - you can come on the Simply More Caravan Travel Package to Bermuda and Mexico, where you'll get your international prescriptions that will allow you to keep buying Simply More - *but not end up here in jail with me."*

WHAT DO I WANT?
SIMPLY MORE

SIMPLY MORE

The ultimate bulking agent

Simply More is not just a product to be bought and sold, but a way of life to be bought and sold.

Founder Hugh Brown

"Friends! Are you ready to sail on the Simply More Travel Package Holiday Caravan Cruise to Mexico and Bermuda? The ship leaves this Saturday. Yes there will be shuttle services. My lawyers have arranged my release on the condition that I stay in the country, but *that's not going to stop me!* Friends, I'm going to be on that ship!

There will be no shortage of Simply More products on this cruise through international waters - not just the basic formulas, but ALL of the others as well; like Simply More with Accelerator when your busy cruise schedule demands it, and Simply More Ladies Formula - the same Simply More quality ingredients, but in a lavender package, Simply More for Dogs, Simply More for Senior Dogs, with life extending Dogjevity or life-shortening Dognity, Simply More with Girth, Simply More with Worms, and Simply More with Girth with Worms with Girth. Don't worry friends, I'll see you on that cruise!"

WHAT DO I WANT?

SIMPLY MORE

The Metro Daily Times Gazette Bulgler

When you've got to know, you know where you've got to go

ALL ABOARD THE PRINCESS BEHEMOTH

The Simply More Travel Package Holiday Caravan Cruise to Mexico and Bermuda aboard the Princess Behemoth is turning into quite a celebrity showcase. Steg Progsten and Steve Climber (pictured here) were spotted as they made their way onboard. Stu Cranstence, Lorb Lorbson, Hundus and Furundus, Bolus Brown, Dr. Soily Kruebens, Rootsin Toobers and Ann Thusiast are all on the passenger list, among many others.

Simply More founder Hugh Brown, who was recently released from jail, has not yet been spotted. Law enforcement officials have been on alert ever since Brown indicated he would not abide by the stipulations of his release. There is a heavy police presence in the area.

Forklifts are still working around the clock loading pallet after pallet of Simply More, Juggernaut medicines and over 3000 kegs of Cren beer, which have been specially brewed for the first time for this cruise. Cren beer has never actually been available to the public even though they have quite a successful advertising campaign with a very catchy song. Cren beer was so inspired by Hugh Brown's personal story that they decided to finally actually brew some Cren. They have also included 800 kegs of Cren infused with Simply More with Accelerator just for the Simply More enthusiasts that will be on board.

SIMPLY MORE
The ultimate bulking agent

Friends, I'm free!

Founder Hugh Brown

"I have just been released from jail, and I'm on the way to the Princess Behemoth and the Simply More Caravan Travel Package to Bermuda and Mexico, and I hope you're coming too. I've told you my story and today I want to hear yours, as we meet at the dock where the Princess Behemoth gets ready to sail.

Friends, it's a great day. Create giant human pyramids on every hilltop. Give birth to children and bring them to that Caravan Cruise. Set fire to buildings so that the smoke rising from the destruction and the corpses will be the last thing we see as we sail into the sunset."

WHAT DO I WANT?
SIMPLY MORE

(Hugh Brown has been released pending legal proceeding. He is not allowed to leave the country for any reason. Law enforcement officials will be waiting at the ship to re-arrest Mr. Brown if needed.)

Chapter Nine

Brought to you by the law offices of Ernst Ernst Ernst & Ernst

At Juggernaut Pharmaceuticals we're working to gain your trust, so that we can take over the world. Won't you join us?

𝕿𝕳𝖊 𝕸𝖊𝖙𝖗𝖔 𝕯𝖆𝖎𝖑𝖞 𝕿𝖎𝖒𝖊𝖘 𝕲𝖆𝖟𝖊𝖙𝖙𝖊 𝕭𝖚𝖑𝖌𝖑𝖊𝖗

When you've got to know, you know where you've got to go

THE PRINCESS BEHEMOTH SAILS! NO SIGN OF BROWN

The Simply More Travel Package Holiday Caravan Cruise to Mexico and Bermuda aboard the Princess Behemoth has left port without the recently released Simply More magnate, Hugh Brown. Brown had vowed that he would be on the cruise, defying court orders that he remain in the country awaiting trial on numerous civil and criminal racketeering charges.

Over the past few days Brown has been sending apocalyptic messages to his followers, including messages that some have seen as incitements to violence.

There was heavy police presence at the dock as there were concerns that the massive crowds that had gathered would turn ugly.

The cruise was sold out, leaving many agitated people on the dock. One frustrated man was concerned about how he was going to purchase more Simply More, now that the entire world inventory was on the ship that just left port. "I'm running low here," he said. "How are we supposed to get more of the stuff?"

The Metro Daily Times Gazette Bugler has a reporter on board and she reported that the crowd on the dock had swelled to what looked like over 10,000 people who were chanting Simply More slogans, with some jumping in the water in an attempt to get around the police lines.

LET'S GET IT OFF!
WITH HUNDUS AND FURUNDUS

Join Hundus and Furundus on board the Princess Behemoth as they show you self-defense techniques you won't believe.
Your fat doesn't stand a chance.
Watch in amazement as they show off their martial arts moves. Let these two fitness gurus show you how to lose the fat the old fashioned way - **one pound at a time!** Get pumped as you follow along with their unusual form and techniques. So wake up early with Hundus and Furundus and

start losing it!

Look for the Hundus and Furundus on the upper deck on the Princess Behemoth every morning at 4:30

The Metro Daily Times Gazette Bulgler

When you've got to know, you know where you've got to go

LORBSON SPOUTS SCAT CROWD STAMPEDES

Just as the voyage of the Princess Behemoth was getting underway there was an incident in the Juggernaut Theatre. Lorb Lorbson had just started singing his scat version of "The Way We Were" as part of the **Welcome Aboard!** entertainment series when the crowd inside the theatre starting running for the exits.

The Juggernaut Theatre

Only the starboard exits were open which caused everyone to move in that direction in an effort to get out of the theatre as quickly as possible. Seeing that the Juggernaut Theatre is on one of the upper decks of the ship, the sudden re-distribution of weight caused the ship to list noticeably to starboard.

The crew finally got people calmed down when they told the passengers that Lorb Lorbson's performance would end soon. However, since then the ship has continued to lean, and there is speculation that the listing ship may have caused some of the enormous load of Simply More, Juggernaut medicines, Pet Chef dog food, and the hundreds of kegs of Cren beer

Lorb Lorbson

down in the hold to shift. Crews are venturing into the hold now to assess any possible damage and see if they can get the ship back to a fully upright position.

𝕿𝖍𝖊 𝕸𝖊𝖙𝖗𝖔 𝕯𝖆𝖎𝖑𝖞 𝕿𝖎𝖒𝖊𝖘 𝕲𝖆𝖟𝖊𝖙𝖙𝖊 𝕭𝖚𝖑𝖌𝖑𝖊𝖗

When you've got to know, you know where you've got to go

HUGH AND BOLUS BROWN ARRIVE BY HELICOPTER!

The Simply More founder and his son Bolus have arrived at the Princess Behemoth in dramatic fashion. They were brought by helicopter once the ship was safely out in international waters. The fact that the ship is still listing to starboard and the heavy swells and stiff wind made for a dangerous operation. The helicopter hovered above the upper pool deck for many tense minutes as crowds of passengers gathered. The people cheered loudly as Brown and his son were finally lowered onto the rolling ship.

The eccentric billionaire bulking agent magnate was then quickly whisked away by personal security guards and taken to the Emperor Suite on the uppermost deck of the ship.

Hugh Brown

Bolus Brown

STRAP ON
the Flextrek 37,000,000,000,000 and start *POUNDING AWAY* at Mother Nature!

She may resist, but Mother Nature doesn't stand a chance.

ARCHWOOD

𝕿𝖍𝖊 𝕸𝖊𝖙𝖗𝖔 𝕯𝖆𝖎𝖑𝖞 𝕿𝖎𝖒𝖊𝖘 𝕲𝖆𝖟𝖊𝖙𝖙𝖊 𝕭𝖚𝖑𝖌𝖑𝖊𝖗

When you've got to know, you know where you've got to go

TROUBLE DOWN BELOW FOR THE PRINCESS BEHEMOTH

Crew members have reached the storage compartments deep in the hold of the ship and they report a chaotic scene down there. The crew had trouble getting into the storage area as the jumbled contents were blocking the entry.

When they were able to open the hatch they saw that dozens of kegs of Cren Beer infused with Simply More with Accelerator have tipped over and broken open, soaking pallets of Vitryol, Lethalis, and Simply More with Worms with Girth. The leaning of the ship has caused numerous other pallets to fall over and break open and are now in a jumbled heap. Many other Simply More boxes and cans of Pet Chef with Dogjevity and Dognity have also been breached and are now soaking up the Cren Beer. This is creating a sludge pile that seems to be growing, according to the one crew member who ventured inside. Concerns are being raised as to what kind of chemical reactions might be taking place as the spilled cargo mixes together. Already there are fumes being produced and exhaust fans have been brought in to try and clear the air below decks. Request for more information from Juggernaut Pharmaceuticals, Cren Beer, Pet Chef, and Simply More about the possible hazards in this situation have gone unanswered.

Cruise Director Brandon sent this message over the loudspeaker. "We are working on this problem, we can assure you," he said. "Crew members working hard to remedy this situation. In the mean time there are plenty of activities on board to keep you busy and you won't want to miss any of it!"

Activities include Steve Climber modeling the new French Wedge Le Crevasse edition on the pool deck at 3pm and Stu Cranstence lecturing on 'Areas' in the library at 4pm. Juggernaut Pharmaceutical representatives will also be giving out free samples of Vytriol on the Lido deck all day.

T𝔥e Metro Daily Times Gazette Bulgler

When you've got to know, you know where you've got to go

UNKNOWN CREATURES IN THE BOWELS OF THE PRINCESS!

The Simply More Travel Package Holiday Caravan Cruise to Mexico and Bermuda aboard the Princess Behemoth has already been plagued with trouble, but now an even more ominous situation has developed. A crew member who was attempting to clean up the spillage down in the hold came back out looking pale and frightened. He was asked about what he saw, but he speaks no English. Through interpreters they were finally able to find out that he saw creatures in amongst the wreckage. The interpreter said that the crew member referred to them as "white snakes" and said that they were "eating the stuff." The crew member was able to get one dark photograph of the creatures but it is not clear from the photo what kind of animal this is.

The man has refused to go back in the hold, and they are currently trying to find someone else who is willing to go in there to assess what is happening. The other crew members from his remote island have refuse to go in the hold.

The Metro Daily Times Gazette Bugler has repeatedly asked Juggernaut Pharmaceuticals and Simply More for information on what might happen if this mixture of medications and bulking agents were to be ingested by some kind of snake, with no response. Stu Cranstence, who is known as an authority on Juggernaut medications, was asked about the possible dangers. "As long as they don't eat Skinflair-trynsol and Sklinflairtrynsol at the same time, it should be okay," said Cranstence. "Although if they got into the Vytriol...I don't know. That one's new. It doesn't have a track record. I don't think they even know the side effects yet."

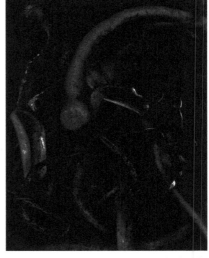

Photo of unknown creatures in the hold

Holiday Caravan Cruises

A Message from Captain Nordingdale Whipscrit
For immediate release:

Greetings passengers on board the Princess Behemoth. As you may have noticed, the ship is currently listing around 15 degrees to starboard. This was caused by a stampede of passengers on the upper deck which in turn caused some of the cargo down in the hold to shift, which is why we are still heeling over. The Princess has a high center of gravity and that has exacerbated the problem.

In an attempt to remedy the heeling, we sent crew members down to re-stow and secure the cargo. Unfortunately this operation was interrupted when it was discovered that there were creatures in the hold consuming the spilled cargo. Upon further investigation it was determined that the creatures are in fact a species of kelp. After reviewing security footage from the dock, it appears that a pregnant female may have followed a passenger to the dock and then stowed away inside a pallet of Lethalis.

This female has since given birth to scores of kelplings and they are currently feeding voraciously on the spilled cargo in the hold. They have become extremely aggressive and will strike at anyone who comes near them.

I would like to reassure passengers that the kelp are safely secured behind locked doors. **There is no need for panic.**

We are working on a solution to the kelp problem, but right now the issue of the heeling ship is our main priority.

Thank you for your patience as we address these matters. As thanks for your patience I have authorized **3 free alcoholic drinks** for anyone attending Lorb Lorbson's encore performance in the Juggernaut Theatre on the top deck this evening at 9pm. I hope you will all come up and enjoy a couple of drinks on me and watch the show.

The Metro Daily Times Gazette Bulgler

When you've got to know, you know where you've got to go

LORBSON THROWS DOWN SCAT
PASSENGERS FLEE!

Just as the passengers on board the Princess Behemoth were at their wit's end dealing with the listing ship, crooner Lorb Lorbson has stepped up and has emerged as a hero.

Lorbson had just started his scat version of "After the Lovin" in the very crowded Juggernaut Theatre when passengers again rushed for the exits. This time the staff had the only the port exits open.

The Juggernaut Theatre

The stampeding passengers ran for the port exits and the railing beyond, causing the ship to roll in an arc and then lean in the opposite direction. Crew members then herded the passengers back towards the middle of the ship by promising a DJ party by the pool with prizes for the best dancers and free chicken strips.

The ship sloshed back and forth a few times, but finally came to an equilibrium.

Credit for this plan is due mainly to Captain Nordingdale Whipscrit who came up with the idea after watching security video footage of the original incident. His plan has worked and the ship is now back in a fully upright position. Many thanks to the Captain and crew for a well executed plan, and thanks to Lorb Lorbson for his special ability to move people.

Lorb Lorbson

Holiday Caravan Cruises

A Message from Captain Nordingdale Whipscrit
For immediate release:

Greetings passengers. As you have surely noticed, the operation to right the ship was a success. We apologize for any inconvenience caused by the ship rocking back and forth to such a degree, but we are safely upright and stable and are steaming ahead on our cruise.

Unfortunately the violent rocking of the ship has caused the remaining undamaged cargo of Cren, Juggernaut medicines, Simply More and Pet Chef products in the hold to break open and mix together. Security footage from inside the hold shows that the contents have now fully mixed together into a thick sludge. We do not currently believe that this mix of substances poses a risk to passengers.

As far as the kelp are concerned, security footage shows no more signs of the creatures in the hold. We are not sure if all of the kelp perished during the sloshing phase or if some of them survived. Crew members are investigating the situation. There is concern that they may have gotten access to the ventilation or sewage systems. Until we get an idea of whether the kelp died or have survived and are currently hiding somewhere else on the ship, we ask that passengers remain vigilant and report any unusual activity to crew members.

There is no need for alarm or panic as the crew are searching the ship from top to bottom and we will locate the kelp shortly.

In the meantime, enjoy the cruise. We will soon be passing by some picturesque uninhabited islands that will able to be seen from the port side of the Princess. Please enjoy yourselves. There is also bingo and karaoke later tonight.

𝕿𝕳𝖊 𝕸𝖊𝖙𝖗𝖔 𝕯𝖆𝖎𝖑𝖞 𝕿𝖎𝖒𝖊𝖘 𝕲𝖆𝖟𝖊𝖙𝖙𝖊 𝕭𝖚𝖑𝖌𝖑𝖊𝖗

When you've got to know, you know where you've got to go

KILLER KELP CAUSE PALPABLE PANIC

Despite a reassuring message from Captain Nordingdale Whipscrit, passengers on board the Princess Behemoth have begun to panic as the killer kelp have made it into the ventilation system and are emerging from the air ducts.

Last nights bingo game on the 27th deck was disrupted when several kelp dropped out of the ceiling ducts and started thrashing around. The bingo room emptied quickly with the kelp in hot pursuit. Passengers ran into the karaoke bar but were greeted by more kelp dropping out of the ceiling. This caused a stampede of screaming passengers to run out to the open decks.

The kelp seem to be coming from everywhere. Multiple injuries from falls and kelp stings have sent people to the infirmary which is now full to overflowing. The kelp seem to be searching for someone or something in particular and are now roaming the halls.

An announcement over the PA advised people to stay in their staterooms and block the ventilation ducts until further notice.

A large group of kelp were found nesting inside Steve Climber's Flextrek 37,000,000,000,000 Whipsnake Edition when passengers noticed that the enormous backpack - which is on display on the Promenade deck - began to writhe.

Crew members have been frantically trying to calm passengers while attempting to catch and contain the kelp. The crew member's inability to speak or understand English has made communication quite difficult and has resulted in many misunderstandings. The crew have begun using hand signals that imitate the writhing of the kelp to try and warn passengers about areas that are currently infested with the creatures.

The safest place at the moment seems to be out on the open decks where people have resorted to protecting themselves from the striking kelp with cushions from the lounge chairs.

As of this writing the kelp seem to be concentrating their activities on deck 23 in the hallway near the port cabins. There is a currently a writhing cluster of them completely blocking the passageway.

Holiday Caravan Cruises

A Message from Captain Nordingdale Whipscrit
For immediate release:

Greetings passengers. As you may have noticed, the kelp from the hold have gained access to the rest of the ship through the ventilation system. The kelp have now spread throughout the Princess Behemoth. It has become clear that the kelp are in search of one particular passenger who we have identified as Steg Prongsten. The kelp have been gathering outside of Prongsten's cabin in an attempt to reach and possibly attack him.

At first light tomorrow we are going to start an operation to rid the ship of the kelp. Prongsten has bravely agreed to help us with this risky operation. We are going to create a diversion in the hallway to allow Prongsten to emerge from his cabin and proceed down the hall and to a lower deck where we will get him onto a launch. We will make sure that the kelp see him getting in the boat.

This high speed launch will then race to an uninhabited island and deposit Prongsten on the shore. The plan is that Prongsten will then run the entire length of the island, luring the kelp behind him. Once he reaches the north end of the island, the launch will pick him up and deliver him back to the ship.

If all goes well the kelp will be marooned on the island. Any stragglers still on board the ship will then be dealt with.

Prongsten has assured us that he can outrun the kelp. We are grateful to him for his willingness to help with this operation.

We appreciate your patience as we attempt to rid the ship of this menace. As a token of our appreciation, (if Prongsten is successful), we will have a party on the Lido deck with free alcohol from 5:00 - 5:30. Please enjoy responsibly.

𝕿𝖍𝖊 𝕸𝖊𝖙𝖗𝖔 𝕯𝖆𝖎𝖑𝖞 𝕿𝖎𝖒𝖊𝖘 𝕲𝖆𝖟𝖊𝖙𝖙𝖊 𝕭𝖚𝖑𝖌𝖑𝖊𝖗

When you've got to know, you know where you've got to go

PRONGSTEN PREVAILS!

Steg Prongsten has lived up to his own hype and proven that he is in fact a world-class athlete. Today he thrilled the passengers on board the Princess Behemoth with a performance that is one for the record books.

Prongsten got into the launch and was lowered to the water as the kelp followed him, slithering over the railing in hot pursuit. The launch raced away towards an uninhabited island with the kelp close behind. Once he hit the sand, Prongsten did a few stretches as he waited for the kelp to catch up. He then took off in his signature hunch-backed style, racing down the beach.

Passengers on board watched from the railing through binoculars and screamed in horror as the kelp gained on him. It appeared he was going to be overcome by the angry hissing mob of kelp, but that's when Prongsten kicked it into high gear. The race was too close to call as they sped down the deserted beach, but Prongsten started to pull away. He had gained some ground by the time he reached the north end of the island and dove into the waiting launch.

The frustrated kelp collapsed in exhaustion and lay on the beach in a tangled heap as the launch whisked him back to the ship where he was given a hero's reception from the passengers.

When people remarked at how calm he was Prongsten said, "I'm a world-class athlete. I travel the globe looking for the ultimate settings to train and test the limits of human fitness. Do really think I'm going to be afraid of some damn seaweed?"

The Princess now appears to be completely kelp-free much to the relief of all on board.

SIMPLY MORE

The ultimate bulking agent

We're moving on to an exciting new world!

Founder Hugh Brown

"Friends, this is Hugh Brown. Some people might say that what has happened in the cargo hold of the Princess Behemoth is a **tragedy**, but we are choosing to think of it as an **opportunity**. In an exciting new collaboration with Juggernaut Pharmaceuticals, Pet Chef, and Cren beer, Simply More is introducing a revolutionary new product we are calling *The Ultimate Elixir.*

Passengers are encouraged to follow the signs down to the cargo hold and bring empty water bottles or any other container you can find, and fill them with *The Ultimate Elixir*. Customers will be charged a reasonable fee based on liquid volume. Concerns have been raised about the fact that the elixir contains life-shortening Dognity, but don't worry about that, as it also contains an equal amount of life-extending Dogjevity. Some may question whether it is safe to combine all of the Juggernaut medicines in this way, especially Skinflairtrynsol and Sklinflairtrynsol, but representatives of Juggernaut assure me that the product presents no immediate harm to consumers."

WHAT DO I WANT?

SIMPLY MORE

(Lawyers from the offices of Ernst, Ernst, Ernst, & Ernst will be on hand to handle conditional release forms to ensure no liability for any of the companies involved.)

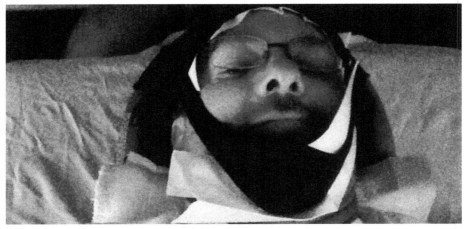

Holiday Caravan Cruises

A Message from Captain Nordingdale Whipscrit
For immediate release.

Greetings passengers. This voyage of the Princess Behemoth has presented many challenges and we have risen together to overcome all of the obstacles, but there is another challenge ahead for us. A low pressure system has developed directly in our projected route. It is predicted that overnight it will become the 9th hurricane of the season and will be named Iyana.

Due to the unusually high profile of the Princess Behemoth, extreme caution will be taken with regards to our planned route and strategy to deal with the projected high winds and large swells.

We are asking passengers to remain alert and follow all instructions as we prepare for this storm. The storm's position and projected path make it nearly impossible for us to avoid completely. We don't have sufficient speed to outrun the storm or circle around it. We have decided instead to try to take the least dangerous route, attempting to keep our bow to the wind at all times.

Passengers are encouraged to keep their life jackets close by and keep in mind where your muster stations are in case we have a loss of engine power or steering. The crew will be busy moving heavy objects down to the promenade deck to lower our center of gravity. This means the shopping area will be closed until we make it through the storm. We apologize for this inconvenience.

It's time to literally batten down the hatches, but I am confident that together we can weather this storm. Because of the intense nature of preparations and the possible loss of communications, this will be last official message we send. Communication with the outside world will be cut off shortly due to the intense weather, so hold on and we will talk again when we emerge from hurricane Iyana.

Over and out!

At Juggernaut Pharmaceuticals we're doing just one thing, saving all life on earth.

Announcing a new all-in-one product

The Ultimate Elixir

These four dynamic companies have joined forces to create a product the likes of which humanity has never seen. It's everything you want and need.

The ultimate bulking agent

The Ultimate Elixir has not been approved for human use. Contains 5.2% alcohol by volume. Dosages of the Ultimate Elixir have not been calculated.

Side effects may include: Vague feelings of unease, rapid snap-coiling of the penis, giant eye-maggots, explosive bowel movements, supersonic flatulence, multiple facial scrotums, crotch coral, weak stream, strong stream, cauliflower-shaped growths on the anus and face. Men taking the Ultimate Elixir may notice their penis taking on the appearance of stool. The FDA is still evaluating all of the possible side effects.

𝕿𝖍𝖊 𝕸𝖊𝖙𝖗𝖔 𝕯𝖆𝖎𝖑𝖞 𝕿𝖎𝖒𝖊𝖘 𝕲𝖆𝖟𝖊𝖙𝖙𝖊 𝕭𝖚𝖌𝖑𝖊𝖗

When you've got to know, you know where you've got to go

NO WORD FROM THE PRINCESS BEHEMOTH

The Metro Daily Times Gazette Bugler's reporter on board the Princess Behemoth cruise ship sent out her last message over 12 hours ago shortly before they entered hurricane Iyana off the Mexican coast. Since then there have been no communications received and no signs of the ship's whereabouts. No SOS signals were received by other vessels in the area.

It is still unclear at this time if the ship sank with all hands on board, or if it was crippled in the storm and managed to find shelter, or if there is some other explanation of the disappearance of this gigantic cruise ship. Search and rescue teams have been dispatched to the area, but it will take at least 12 more hours until they reach the ship's last reported location.

A marine architect we talked to speculates that a ship with that high of a profile would have great difficulty handling the winds speeds and wave heights that have been recorded with this storm. Iyana has gone through a rapid intensification in the area where the Princess Behemoth is believed to be. Satellite images show the eye of the storm is now very well defined and readings showed that the atmospheric pressure has dropped drastically within the last few hours. Top winds speeds are now estimated to be 180-200 mph making Iyana a strong category 5 major hurricane.

Iyana is a massive and dangerous storm. Unfortunately its forward motion has now slowed, complicating any rescue attempts and obscuring attempts to get visual sightings from the air.

If the ship indeed sinks, this would be the greatest shipping disaster in history with a potential of over 20,000 lives lost.

The next 12-24 hours will tell if the Princess Behemoth survives the storm or not.

The Metro Daily Times Gazette Bulgler

When you've got to know, you know where you've got to go

THE PRINCESS SURVIVES!

After being out of communications for over 24 hours, the Princess Behemoth has made contact with authorities and reports that while the ship sustained some damage, it has survived the hurricane.

Our reporter on board says that the ship was saved by last minute maneuvering by Captain Nordingdale Whipscrit. After looking over the latest satellite imagery of hurri-

Waves from hurricane Iyana batter offshore rocks

cane Iyana, the captain changed course and, for the first time on this voyage, turned on the effluent jets in the stern of the ship to add speed. They were then able to race for a group of offshore islands, one of which had high cliffs to offer some break from the screaming winds.

As the wind changed direction the captain used his skill and experience to keep the bow to the tempest and avoid the offshore rocks and reefs. It was a nail-biting 24 hours of battering winds and risky maneuvers. The captain repeatedly used the effluent jets to maintain position.

Passengers kept themselves occupied by sampling the Ultimate Elixir and comparing notes on its effects. The captain credits the Ultimate Elixir and its explosiveness for giving the ship an impressive 10 additional knots over the ship's top rated speed.

"I was skeptical, but those jets really came through for us," said Whipscrit. "We would not have made it to those sheltering islands if it wasn't for that stuff. It's like rocket fuel."

Princess Behemoth will now continue on its way to Bermuda.

Back on the mainland, authorities have dropped all charges against Hugh Brown in light of the heroic impact his formulas had on the saving of the vessel and all hands on board. Simply More products, including the Ultimate Elixir, have now been re-certified and will be widely available for purchase once again. Juggernaut Pharmaceuticals was also rewarded with a full certification to begin selling their products again. Juggernaut has announced that they will be featuring the Princess Behemoth on its new packaging of The Ultimate Elixir. A massive rally has been arranged for when the ship reaches its home port again.

Were you injured by explosive bowel movements after taking the Ultimate Elixir and almost killed by a hurricane on the The Simply More Travel Package Holiday Caravan Cruise to Mexico and Bermuda on board the Princess Behemoth?

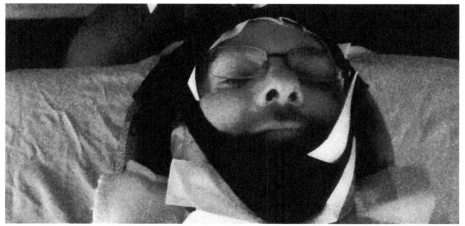

Actual passenger still undergoing extensive ongoing treatment

If so, you may be eligible for financial compensation.

$$$$$$$$$$$$$

Contact the law offices of Ernst Ernst Ernst & Ernst immediately for information that will get you the help you deserve. All of our clients are people like you who are seeking financial relief to pay for the astronomical medical costs suffered after taking the Ultimate Elixir during this recent disastrous cruise.

CALL NOW!

1 (555)-ERNSTERNSTERNSTANDERNST

The law offices of
ERNST ERNST ERNST & ERNST

Acknowledgments

Many thanks to all of the people who have contributed to this digest. Tavis Gustafson has been an invaluable member of the team and appears here as Dr. Soily Cruebens. Gaia Rhodes has been a true soldier on our many outings. Others who need to be thanked and who appear in these pages are: Aylee Rhodes, Jelani Felix, Bret Bostock, Mark Woodley, Rebecca King-Young, Henry Young, Taco, Mark Barry, and Jonathan Rose. Several dogs need to be mentioned as well - thanks to Maverick, Cash, Strawber, Cali and Dexter. The vast majority of the photos were taken by myself with contributions from Azi Ali, Michael Longstaff, Tavis Gustafson, Naomi Pitcairn, Jelani Felix and Roberto Ibarra. All of the graphics and photo editing were done by myself.

Owen Rose

Here is a list of our YouTube videos featured in the digest (arranged by date uploaded)

Flextrek 37 Trillion
Flextrek's Augmenteon
Lorb Lorbson Live at the Cheripintera
Cren beer commercial
Wolfheart cologne for men
Hundus and Furundus
The Flextrek 37 Trillion Gravitrex
Let's Get it Off!
Jumping Jack Technique
The Fart Workout
Amazing Backpack Technology
The French Wedge
Announcing Stryreechlinstral
Soundcheck at the Cheripintera
Kelp
Let's Ask Stu, Feff has a question
Lorb sings Higher Ground by Stevie Wonder
Lethalis
Juggernaut releases Poisantin
Juggernaut releases Pandemical
Lorb Lorbson: Up close and personal
Pandemical Update
Introducing Steg Prongsten
The Flextrek Clic Method
Panacea: The Superbowl Ad
Stu on Bone Sticks
Lorb Lorbson Sings!
The French Wedge (full version)
Stu on Wind
Steg Prongsten battles kelp
Old pappy has a question
The Juggernaut Pharmaceutical collection
Multiple Ernst Ernst Ernst & Ersnt commercials
Can your backpack do this?
The Flextrek Whipsnake
Pathagen
Stu on avalanches
Myscleetra
Skinflairtrynsol for Everyone
Stu Cranstence out in the field again
Steve Climber by TheFergusShow

There are many other videos on our **doctorodub** YouTube Channel. Please feel free to browse them at your leisure.